YOUR PERSONAL

ASTROLOGY

PLANNER

VIRGO
2009

YOUR PERSONAL
ASTROLOGY
PLANNER

VIRGO
2009

RICK LEVINE **& JEFF** JAWER

STERLING

New York / London
www.sterlingpublishing.com

STERLING and the distinctive Sterling logo are registered
trademarks of Sterling Publishing Co., Inc.

2   4   6   8   10   9   7   5   3   1

Published by Sterling Publishing Co., Inc.
387 Park Avenue South, New York, NY 10016
© 2008 by Sterling Publishing Co., Inc.
Text © 2008 Rick Levine and Jeff Jawer
Distributed in Canada by Sterling Publishing
c/o Canadian Manda Group, 165 Dufferin Street
Toronto, Ontario, Canada M6K 3H6
Distributed in the United Kingdom by GMC Distribution Services
Castle Place, 166 High Street, Lewes, East Sussex, England BN7 1XU
Distributed in Australia by Capricorn Link (Australia) Pty. Ltd.
P.O. Box 704, Windsor, NSW 2756, Australia

Manufactured in the United States of America
All rights reserved

Sterling ISBN 978-1-4027-5035-9

For information about custom editions, special sales, premium and
corporate purchases, please contact Sterling Special Sales
Department at 800-805-5489 or
specialsales@sterlingpublishing.com.

TABLE OF CONTENTS

THE PURPOSE OF THIS BOOK

The more you learn about yourself, the better able you are to wisely use the energies in your life. For more than 3,000 years, astrology has been the sharpest tool in the box for describing the human condition. Used by virtually every culture on the planet, astrology continues to serve as a link between individual lives and planetary cycles. We gain valuable insights into personal issues with a birth chart, and can plot the patterns of the year ahead in meaningful ways for individuals as well as groups. You share your sun sign with eight percent of humanity. Clearly, you're not all going to have the same day, even if the basic astrological cycles are the same. Your individual circumstances, the specific factors of your entire birth chart, and your own free will help you write your unique story.

The purpose of this book is to describe the energies of the Sun, Moon, and planets for the year ahead and help you create your future, rather than being a victim of it. We aim to facilitate your journey by showing you the turns ahead in the road of life and hopefully the best ways to navigate them.

YOU ARE THE STAR
OF YOUR LIFE

It is not our goal to simply predict events. Rather, we are reporting the planetary energies—the cosmic weather in which you are living—so that you understand these conditions and know how to use them most effectively.

The power, though, isn't in the stars, but in your mind, your heart, and the choices that you make every day. Regardless of how strongly you are buffeted by the winds of change or bored by stagnation, you have many ways to view any situation. Learning about the energies of the Sun, Moon, and planets will both sharpen and widen your perspective, thereby giving you additional choices.

The language of astrology is a gift of awareness, not a rigid set of rules. It works best when blended with common sense, intuition, and self-trust. This is your life, and no one knows how to live it as well as you. Take what you need from this book and leave the rest. Although the planets set the stage for the year ahead, you're the writer, director, and star of your life and you can play the part in whatever way you choose. *Your Personal Astrology Planner* uses information about your sun sign to give you a better understanding of how the planetary waves will wash upon your shore. We each navigate our lives through time, and each moment has unique qualities. Astrology gives us the ability to describe the constantly changing timescape. For example, if you know the trajectory and the speed of an approaching storm, you can choose to delay a leisurely afternoon sail on the bay, thus avoiding an unpleasant situation.

By reading this book, you can improve your ability to align with the cosmic weather, the larger patterns that affect you day to day. You can become more effective by aligning with the cosmos and cocreating the year ahead with a better understanding of the energies around you.

Astrology doesn't provide quick fixes to life's complex issues. It doesn't offer neatly packed black-and-white answers in a world filled with an infinite variety of shapes and colors. It can, however, give you a much clearer picture of the invisible forces influencing your life.

ENERGY & EVENTS

Two sailboats can face the same gale yet travel in opposite directions as a result of how the sails are positioned. Similarly, how you respond to the energy of a particular set of circumstances may be more responsible for your fate than the given situation itself. We delineate the energetic winds for your year ahead, but your attitude shapes the unfolding events, and your responses alter your destiny.

This book emphasizes the positive, not because all is good, but because astrology shows us ways to transform even the power of a storm into beneficial results. Empowerment comes from learning to see the invisible energy patterns that impact the visible landscape as you fill in the details of your story every day on this spinning planet, orbited by the Moon, lit by the Sun, and colored by the nuances of the planets.

You are a unique point in an infinite galaxy of unlimited possibilities, and the choices that you make have consequences. So use this book in a most magical way to consciously improve your life.

MOON CHARTS

2009 NEW MOONS

Each New Moon marks the beginning of a cycle. In general, this is the best time to plant seeds for future growth. Use the days preceeding the New Moon to finish old business prior to starting what comes next. The focused mind can be quite sharp during this phase. Harness the potential of the New Moon by stating your intentions—out loud or in writing—for the weeks ahead. Hold these goals in your mind; help them grow to fruition through conscious actions as the Moon gains light during the following two weeks. In the chart below, the dates and times refer to when the Moon and Sun align in each zodiac sign (see p16), initiating a new lunar cycle.

DATE	TIME	SIGN
January 26	2:55 AM EST	Aquarius (ECLIPSE)
February 24	8:35 PM EST	Pisces
March 26	12:06 PM EDT	Aries
April 24	11:23 PM EDT	Taurus
May 24	8:11 AM EDT	Gemini
June 22	3:35 PM EDT	Cancer
July 21	10:35 PM EDT	Cancer (ECLIPSE)
August 20	6:02 AM EDT	Leo
September 18	2:44 PM EDT	Virgo
October 18	1:33 AM EDT	Libra
November 16	2:14 PM EST	Scorpio
December 16	7:02 AM EST	Sagittarius

2009 FULL MOONS

The Full Moon reflects the light of the Sun as subjective feelings reflect the objective events of the day. Dreams seem bigger; moods feel stronger. The emotional waters run with deeper currents. This is the phase of culmination, a turning point in the energetic cycle. Now it's time to listen to the inner voices. Rather than starting new projects, the two weeks after the Full Moon are when we complete what we can and slow our outward expressions in anticipation of the next New Moon. In this chart, the dates and times refer to when the moon is opposite the sun in each zodiac sign, marking the emotional peak of each lunar cycle.

DATE	TIME	SIGN
January 10	10:27 PM EST	Cancer
February 9	9:49 AM EST	Leo (ECLIPSE)
March 10	10:38 PM EDT	Virgo
April 9	10:56 AM EDT	Libra
May 9	12:01 AM EDT	Scorpio
June 7	2:12 PM EDT	Sagittarius
July 7	5:21 AM EDT	Capricorn (ECLIPSE)
August 5	8:55 PM EDT	Aquarius (ECLIPSE)
September 4	12:03 PM EDT	Pisces
October 4	2:10 AM EDT	Aries
November 2	2:14 PM EST	Taurus
December 2	2:30 AM EST	Gemini
December 31	2:12 PM EST	Cancer (ECLIPSE)

ASTROLOGY, YOU & THE WORLD

WELCOME TO YOUR SUN SIGN

The Sun, Moon, and Earth and all the planets lie within a plane called the **ecliptic** and move through a narrow band of stars made up by 12 constellations called the **zodiac**. The Earth revolves around the Sun once a year, but from our point of view, it appears that the Sun moves through each sign of the zodiac for one month. There are 12 months and astrologically there are 12 signs. The astrological months, however, do not match our calendar, and start between the 19th and 23rd of each month. Everyone is born to an astrological month, like being born in a room with a particular perspective of the world. Knowing your sun sign provides useful information about your personality and your future, but for a more detailed astrological analysis, a full birth chart calculation based on your precise date, time, and place of birth is necessary. Get your complete birth chart online at:

http://www.tarot.com/astrology/astroprofile

This book is about your zodiac sign. Your Sun in the earth sign of efficient Virgo is analytical and practical. You excel at separating the wheat from the chaff, the valuable kernel from the rest. As such, you can be highly discriminating, even critical. You're a careful perfectionist in your work. Your greatest strength is being able to apply what you know to serve others. More than anything, you want to be useful.

THE PLANETS

We refer to the Sun and Moon as planets. Don't worry; we do know about modern astronomy. Although the Sun is really a star and the Moon is a satellite, they are called planets for astrological purposes. The astrological planets are the Sun, the Moon, Mercury, Venus, Mars, Jupiter, Saturn, Chiron, Uranus, Neptune, and Pluto.

Your sun sign is the most obvious astrological placement, for the Sun returns to the same sign every year. But at the same time, the Moon is orbiting the Earth, changing signs every two and a third days. Mercury, Venus, and Mars each move through a sign in a few weeks to a few months.

Jupiter spends a whole year in a sign—and Pluto visits a sign for up to 30 years! The ever-changing positions of the planets alter the energetic terrain through which we travel. The planets are symbols; each has a particular range of meanings. For example, Venus is the goddess of love, but it really symbolizes beauty in a spectrum of experiences. Venus can represent romantic love, sensuality, the arts, or good food. It activates anything that we value, including personal possessions and even money. To our ancestors, the planets actually animated life on Earth. In this way of thinking, every beautiful flower contains the essence of Venus.

Each sign has a natural affinity to an individual planet, and as this planet moves through the sky, it sends messages of particular interest to people born under that sign. Your key or ruling planet is Mercury, the Messenger of the Heavens. Quick-silver Mercury is the fastest of the true planets, symbolic of the speed and changeability of thought. Its movement shows the qualities of your thinking process and speech. Planets can be described by many different words, for the mythology of each is a rich tapestry. In this book we use a variety of words when talking about each planet in order to convey the most applicable meaning. The table below describes a few keywords for each planet, including the Sun and Moon.

PLANET	SYMBOL	KEYWORDS
Sun	☉	Consciousness, Will, Vitality
Moon	☽	Subconscious, Emotions, Habits
Mercury	☿	Communication, Thoughts, Transportation
Venus	♀	Desire, Love, Money, Values
Mars	♂	Action, Physical Energy, Drive
Jupiter	♃	Expansion, Growth, Optimism
Saturn	♄	Contraction, Maturity, Responsibility
Chiron	⚷	Healing, Pain, Subversion
Uranus	♅	Awakening, Unpredictable, Inventive
Neptune	♆	Imagination, Spirituality, Confusion
Pluto	♇	Passion, Intensity, Regeneration

HOUSES

Just as planets move through the signs of the zodiac, they also move through the houses in an individual chart. The 12 houses correspond to the 12 signs, but are individualized, based upon your sign. In this book we use Solar Houses, which place your sun sign in your 1st House. Therefore, when a planet enters a new sign it also enters a new house. If you know your exact time of birth, the rising sign determines the 1st House. You can learn your rising sign by entering your birth date at:

http://www.tarot.com/astrology/astroprofile

HOUSE	SIGN	KEYWORDS
1st House	Aries	Self, Appearance, Personality
2nd House	Taurus	Possessions, Values, Self-Worth
3rd House	Gemini	Communication, Siblings, Short Trips
4th House	Cancer	Home, Family, Roots
5th House	Leo	Love, Romance, Children, Play
6th House	Virgo	Work, Health, Daily Routines
7th House	Libra	Marriage, Relationships, Business Partners
8th House	Scorpio	Intimacy, Transformation, Shared Resources
9th House	Sagittarius	Travel, Higher Education, Philosophy
10th House	Capricorn	Career, Community, Ambition
11th House	Aquarius	Groups and Friends, Associations, Social Ideals
12th House	Pisces	Imagination, Spirituality, Secret Activities

ASPECTS

As the planets move through the sky in their various cycles, they form ever-changing angles with one another. Certain angles create significant geometric shapes. So, when two planets are 90 degrees apart, they conform to a square; 60 degrees of separation conforms to a sextile, or six-pointed star. Planets create **aspects** when they're at these special angles. Aspects explain how the individual symbolism of pairs of planets combine into an energetic pattern.

ASPECT	DEGREES	KEYWORDS
Conjunction	0	Compression, Blending, Focus
Opposition	180	Tension, Awareness, Balance
Trine	120	Harmony, Free-Flowing, Ease
Square	90	Resistance, Stress, Dynamic Conflict
Quintile	72	Creativity, Metaphysical, Magic
Sextile	60	Support, Intelligent, Activating
Quincunx	150	Irritation, Annoyance, Adjustment

2009 GENERAL FORECAST:
THE INDIVIDUAL AND THE COLLECTIVE

Astrology works for individuals, groups, and even humanity as a whole. You will have your own story in 2009, but it will unfold among seven billion other tales of human experience in the year ahead. We are each unique, yet our lives touch one another; our destinies are woven together by weather and war, by economy, science, politics, religion, and all the other threads of life on this planet. We make personal choices every day, yet there are great events beyond the control of any one individual. When the power goes out in a neighborhood, it affects everyone, yet individual astrology patterns will describe the personal response of each person. Our existence is both an individual and collective experience.

We are living at a time when the tools of self-awareness fill bookshelves, Web sites, and broad-casts, and we benefit greatly from them. Yet despite all this wisdom, conflicts among groups cause enormous suffering every day. Understanding personal issues is a powerful means for increasing happiness, but knowledge of our collective issues is equally important for our safety, sanity, and well-being. This astrological look at the major trends and planetary patterns for 2009 provides a framework for understanding the potentials and challenges we face together, so that we can advance with tolerance and respect as a community and fulfill our potentials as individuals.

The astrological events used for this forecast are the transits of major planets Jupiter and Saturn, the retrograde cycles of Mercury, and the eclipses of the Sun and the Moon.

A NOTE ABOUT THE DATES IN THIS BOOK

All events are based upon the Eastern Time Zone of the United States. Because of local time differences, an event occurring just minutes after midnight in the East will actually happen the prior day in the rest of the country. Although the key dates are the exact dates of any particular alignment, some of you are so ready for certain things to happen that you can react to a transit a day or two before it is exact. And sometimes you could be so entrenched in habits or unwilling to change that you may not notice the effects right away. Allow extra time around each key date to feel the impact of any event.

JUPITER IN AQUARIUS
COLLECTIVE CONSCIOUSNESS
January 5, 2009–January 17, 2010

Expansive Jupiter enters inventive and idealistic Aquarius, opening our minds to unexpected possibilities and futuristic visions for reorganizing society. Philosophical, religious, and political boundaries are crossed as new combinations of beliefs evolve, replacing outmoded ideologies. The importance of teamwork and cooperation increases as generous Jupiter in group-oriented Aquarius challenges existing hierarchies and dysfunctional authorities. Growing awareness of the interconnectedness of all living creatures favors a holistic view of reality in which environmental issues and unequal distribution of resources can be addressed more effectively.

Jupiter and Aquarius are both associated with mental activity, making this a rich time for breakthroughs in brain research. Practices for developing the mind become popular as baby boomers strive to stay sharp and recent discoveries spur innovative approaches to education. Technology should advance rapidly, especially if it involves networks—an area associated with Aquarius. Yet there is a shadow side to all this intellectual firepower, for both Jupiter and Aquarius have the potential to "know it all." The desire to have all the answers is a driving force for human exploration—even as it can engender hubris and an assumption of infallibility that both negate discussion or compromise. Fortunately, such tendencies are tempered this year by Jupiter's conjunctions with Neptune and Chiron.

Neptune is the planet of compassion and spirituality, representing the boundless field of feeling that lies beyond the limits of the mind. Chiron is the Wounded Healer, a reminder of the value of vulnerability in salving the pain of mortality. Jupiter conjuncts Neptune on May 27, July 10, and December 21 and joins Chiron on May 23, July 22, and December 21. The super-conjunction of Jupiter, Neptune, and Chiron creates a rare mix of awareness on all levels that can go a long way toward opening individual and collective consciousness. We may begin to see ourselves in a new light with greater understanding of our potential and purpose.

SATURN IN VIRGO
LEAVE NO STONE UNTURNED
September 2, 2007–October 29, 2009

Saturn, the planet of boundaries and limitations, takes twenty-nine years to orbit the Sun and pass through all twelve signs of the zodiac. It demands serious responsibility, shows the work needed to overcome obstacles, and teaches us how to build new structures in our lives. Saturn thrives on patience and commitment, rewarding well-planned and persistent effort but punishing sloppiness with delay, disappointment, and failure. Saturn's passage through detail-oriented Virgo is a time to perfect skills, cut waste, and develop healthier habits. Saturn and Virgo are both pragmatic, which makes them an excellent pair for improving the quality of material life. Bodies can be more susceptible to illnesses caused by impure food or water, making this an ideal time to improve your diet. Environmental issues grow in importance as we approach a critical point in the relationship between humanity and planet Earth. Fortunately, Saturn in exacting Virgo is excellent for cleaning up unhealthy toxins produced by old technologies and in leading the way to create new ecologically friendly systems for the future.

Saturn in Virgo highlights flaws and makes it easier to be critical of yourself and others. Yet its true purpose is to solve problems, not simply complain about them. Small steps in a positive direction can slowly build to a tidal wave of improvement wherever you place your attention this year.

SATURN IN LIBRA
TESTING RELATIONSHIPS
October 29, 2009–October 5, 2012

Saturn's shift into peace-loving Libra marks a new chapter in all kinds of relationships. Cooperation and civility allow diplomacy to flourish as reason replaces force. The need to weigh both sides of any argument can slow down personal and public dialogue, yet it's worth the price to build bridges over seemingly impassable chasms. Saturn is "exalted" in Libra according to astrological tradition, suggesting a highly positive link between the planet's principle of integrity and Libra's sense of fair play. The negative side of Saturn, though, is its potential for rigidity, which can manifest now as a stubborn unwillingness to listen. Resistance to opposing points of view is simply a test of their worth; only with careful consideration can they be properly evaluated. Responsible individuals and leaders recognize the importance of treating others as equals as a foundation for any healthy relationship.

MERCURY RETROGRADES
January 11–February 1 in Aquarius / May 2–May 30 in Gemini / September 7–September 29 in Libra

All true planets appear to move retrograde from time to time as a result of being viewed from the moving platform of Earth. The most significant retrograde periods are those of Mercury, the communication planet. Occurring three times a year for roughly three weeks at a time, these are periods when difficulties with details, travel, information flow, and technical matters are likely.

Although Mercury's retrograde phase has received a fair amount of bad press, it isn't necessarily a negative cycle. Because personal and commercial interactions are emphasized, you can actually accomplish more than usual, especially if you stay focused on what needs to be done rather than initiating new projects. But you may feel as if you're treading water—or worse yet, carried backward in an undertow of unfinished business. Worry less about making progress than about the quality of your work. Extra attention should be paid to all your communication exchanges. Avoiding omissions and misunderstandings is the ideal way to preemptively deal with unnecessary complications. Retrograde Mercury is best used to tie up loose ends as you review, redo, reconsider, and, in general, revisit the past.

This year, the three retrogrades are in intellectual air signs (Aquarius, Gemini, and Libra), which can be very useful for analysis and remedial studies that help you reevaluate what you already know so you can take your learning to the next level.

ECLIPSES
Solar: January 26 and July 21
Lunar: February 9, July 7, August 5, and December 31

Solar and Lunar Eclipses are special New and Full
Moons that indicate meaningful changes for individuals
and groups. They are powerful markers of events
whose influences can appear up to three months in
advance and last up to six months afterward.

January 26, Solar Eclipse in Aquarius: Society of the Future

Eclipses are usually about endings, but this one has plenty of propulsion to drive forward new ideas and organizations. Opportunistic Jupiter is conjunct the eclipse to seed minds with vision far into the future. Loving Venus is joined with Uranus, Aquarius's ingenious ruling planet, revealing fresh forms for relationships and uncommon aesthetics. Stern Saturn's opposition to this unconventional pair could stifle expression, but a constructive trine from industrious Mars in Capricorn helps overcome any resistance.

February 9, Lunar Eclipse in Leo: Cosmic Community

A Lunar Eclipse in dramatic Leo cuts egos down to size, turning brilliant stars into black holes and overinflated winners into losers. The appearance of loss, however, may be obscured by nebulous Neptune's conjunction with the Sun and opposition to the Moon, allowing illusion and deception to cover up failures. The upside of this event is an awakening to the connectedness of all living things. Spiritual Neptune in collectivist Aquarius reveals identity beyond personal ego, opening individuals and groups to communities of soul and service. Let pride dissolve in waters of compassion while moving from fields of competition to webs of cooperation. Philosophical Jupiter's close conjunction with the integrative Lunar North Node promises wisdom, while energetic Mars can turn ideas into action.

July 7, Lunar Eclipse in Capricorn: Realigning Responsibilities

This Lunar Eclipse in Capricorn chips away at emotional defenses, revealing gentler ways to manage daily life. The overly ambitious and excessively disciplined may be diverted from their well-defined paths to address personal issues. The usual insecurities associated with an eclipse in traditional Capricorn are lessened by a supportive trine from Saturn. This provides a safety rail of relative stability through this wobbly time. Examine the rules you've created for yourself and consider dropping those that no longer serve your needs. Reducing extraneous obligations can help you focus on the tasks and goals most vital for you right now.

July 21, Solar Eclipse in Cancer: Cutting the Cord

This Solar Eclipse in the last degree of nostalgic Cancer can produce a flood of memories, pulling your attention back to the past. Yet this is no time to linger over photo albums, souvenirs, and thoughts of love found and lost. Say good-bye to self-protective habits that inhibit growth and block fulfillment. Independent Uranus forms a supportive trine to the eclipse, suddenly making it easier to cut loose what's no longer needed. Nurturing the future, rather than the past, is the gift of this significant event. The eclipse is visible in central China and India, making these countries prime candidates for dramatic change.

August 5, Lunar Eclipse in Aquarius: The Kid in You
It's rare that Lunar Eclipses arrive two months in a row, making this summer a period of major transformation. This event in intellectual Aquarius challenges us to come down from ivory towers and act on our innovative ideas. The Sun in bold Leo opposite the Moon indicates the need for courage and a willingness to take risks. Fortunately, assertive Mars in versatile Gemini shows a variety of paths that can lead to success. Quick fixes and last-minute adjustments are easier with a friendly attitude more interested in enjoying the game than in the final score. When heads are made heavy by theory or competition, it's time for the child's heart to appear to bring playfulness to the party.

December 31, Lunar Eclipse in Cancer:
Tough Choices

This Lunar Eclipse in the Moon's own sign of nurturing Cancer can stir deep waters within families and close friendships. Potent Pluto opposes the Moon while strict Saturn squares it, creating tightness and pressure that can be frightening. It's tempting to duck confrontation or avoid any serious change; yet refusing to act only reduces your power. You may have hard choices to make on the cusp of the New Year, but they demand focus and clear intention—powerful allies for redefining life. Sweet Venus in dutiful Capricorn is between Pluto and the Sun, opposite the Moon, tempting you to do anything to maintain appearances. Still, the prizes of fulfillment go to those brave enough to face outer reality and inner desire without flinching.

Remember that all of these astrological events are part of the general cosmic weather for the year, but will affect us each differently based upon our individual astrological signs.

VIRGO
AUGUST–DECEMBER
2008 OVERVIEW

WINDS OF FATE

A dramatic Solar Eclipse in your 12th House of Destiny can jump-start your month with a fateful series of events that have long-lasting consequences. With Mercury and Venus also in your private 12th House, others may not even realize what you're going through now. Venus's entry into Virgo on **August 6,** followed by Mercury on **August 10,** feels a bit like a homecoming, but it's challenging to manage all the planets currently in your sign—the heat of Mars, the responsibility of Saturn, the desires of Venus, and the sharp intelligence of Mercury. There may be too much happening, making it difficult to keep everything under control. You don't have much of a choice, however, when Venus conjoins Saturn on **August 13,** followed by Mercury on **August 15.** Both of these conjunctions stop you in your tracks, forcing you to improve some aspect of yourself that is not up to standards. The Aquarius Full Moon Eclipse on **August 16** overwhelms you with emotions, erasing any lingering doubts about the intensity of these times.

The Sun's entry into efficient Virgo on **August 22** can deliver a boost of brilliance, providing you with much more clarity. The tense opposition from Mercury and Venus to radical Uranus on **August 23** brings the message home; a clean break is surely one of your options. Mercury and Venus enter Libra on **August 28 and August 30,** respectively, reaffirming your desire to bring your life back into balance. A rare second New Moon this month falls in your 1st House of Personality. No matter how much change you have experienced this month, this Virgo New Moon is the stamp of finality that you need in order to move on.

FRIDAY 1 ★ A leap of faith has profound results through tomorrow

SATURDAY 2 ★

SUNDAY 3

MONDAY 4

TUESDAY 5 ★ Postpone decisions until your head clears, after the 6th

WEDNESDAY 6 ★

THURSDAY 7

FRIDAY 8

SATURDAY 9

SUNDAY 10 ★ **SUPER NOVA DAYS** You can't turn back from recent choices

MONDAY 11 ★

TUESDAY 12 ★

WEDNESDAY 13 ★

THURSDAY 14 ★

FRIDAY 15 ★

SATURDAY 16 ★

SUNDAY 17

MONDAY 18

TUESDAY 19

WEDNESDAY 20

THURSDAY 21

FRIDAY 22

SATURDAY 23 ★ Mental fireworks exciting, but pursue only the best ideas

SUNDAY 24

MONDAY 25

TUESDAY 26

WEDNESDAY 27 ★ A change of perspective requires diplomacy through the 28th

THURSDAY 28 ★

FRIDAY 29

SATURDAY 30

SUNDAY 31

CONSOLIDATE YOUR GAINS

September begins on a heavier note as the Sun, now moving through efficient Virgo, makes its annual conjunction with austere Saturn on **September 3.** You must take responsibility for your entire life—the successes and the failures. Last month may have been a wild ride filled with surprise, but it also opened a new path for you. This month, however, is a time of integration, affording you the opportunity to take advantage of what you've learned and to confidently apply this new perspective to your life. The second of three harmonizing trines between optimistic Jupiter and realistic Saturn on **September 8** sets the tone not only for this month, but for the remainder of the year as well. Both Jupiter and Pluto turn direct the same day, fueling this powerful wave of stability. Expanding your life slowly according to your well-organized plans can bring you closer to your idea of personal success while also allowing you greater latitude of self-expression.

In general, your flow of new ideas, as well as any forward progress, may seem slow throughout the month as your ruling planet, Mercury, gradually grinds to a halt, finally turning retrograde on **September 24.** This month is less about breaking new ground than it is about preparing the soil on which you stand for a garden that is yet to be grown. The fantasy-driven Pisces Full Moon on **September 15** can bring a surprising change within a relationship, for it conjuncts unpredictable Uranus in your 7th House of Partnerships. The fair-minded Libra New Moon on **September 29** in your 2nd House of Values is a reminder to consider all perspectives before you decide which ones best fit your principles and personal needs.

MONDAY 1

TUESDAY 2

WEDNESDAY 3 ★ Deliver more than promised to get what you want through the 4th

THURSDAY 4 ★

FRIDAY 5

SATURDAY 6

SUNDAY 7 ★ The antidote to temptation is realism through the 9th

MONDAY 8 ★

TUESDAY 9 ★

WEDNESDAY 10

THURSDAY 11

FRIDAY 12 ★ **SUPER NOVA DAYS** Newfound freedom thrills through the 15th

SATURDAY 13 ★

SUNDAY 14 ★

MONDAY 15 ★

TUESDAY 16

WEDNESDAY 17

THURSDAY 18

FRIDAY 19

SATURDAY 20 ★ Reassess your resources when financial issues emerge
through the 24th

SUNDAY 21 ★

MONDAY 22 ★

TUESDAY 23 ★

WEDNESDAY 24 ★

THURSDAY 25

FRIDAY 26

SATURDAY 27

SUNDAY 28 ★ Let go of logic and indulge your imagination through the 29th

MONDAY 29 ★

TUESDAY 30

YOU ARE WHAT YOU THINK

Mercury the Messenger is not only your key planet but also the key to this whole month. Until **October 15,** Mercury is retracing ground it covered in September, pulling your thoughts back through familiar issues and requiring you to reconsider previous concerns. Mercury spends all of October in Libra the Scales in your 2nd House of Money and Resources, making this a time to balance your accounts and put your possessions in order. Using diplomatic finesse to discover common ground in the midst of conflict eases tensions and strengthens your ability to negotiate. Breaks from this pattern occur when Mercury forms an annoying quincunx with conceptually brilliant Uranus on **October 1,** creating such a shock of excitement that you could find yourself in a state of nervous frenzy, making it difficult for you to concentrate on your work. This stimulating aspect is repeated on **October 28,** indicating the need to find calming activities to prevent the stress caused by high anxiety. Mercury squares extravagant Jupiter on **October 6** and again on **October 26,** setting up another theme for the month. A tendency to exaggerate is possible, so remember to make your usual checklist to ground yourself with the important details that you might otherwise overlook.

The competitive Aries Full Moon on **October 14** falls in your 8th House of Shared Resources, reminding you that you must cooperate with others, even if your personal styles are vastly different. The magnetic Scorpio New Moon on **October 28** falls in your 3rd House of Immediate Environment and is energized by Mars's trine to rebellious Uranus, daring you to express yourself in a surprisingly reckless manner.

WEDNESDAY 1

THURSDAY 2

FRIDAY 3

SATURDAY 4 ★ Find balance, or else overindulge through the 6th

SUNDAY 5 ★

MONDAY 6 ★

TUESDAY 7

WEDNESDAY 8

THURSDAY 9

FRIDAY 10 ★ A new perspective soothes relationship conflict through the 11th

SATURDAY 11 ★

SUNDAY 12

MONDAY 13

TUESDAY 14 ★ SUPER NOVA DAYS Let go of self-criticism through the 15th

WEDNESDAY 15 ★

THURSDAY 16

FRIDAY 17

SATURDAY 18 ★ Set habits aside and accept unexpected adventure and love

SUNDAY 19

MONDAY 20

TUESDAY 21

WEDNESDAY 22

THURSDAY 23

FRIDAY 24

SATURDAY 25

SUNDAY 26

MONDAY 27

TUESDAY 28

WEDNESDAY 29

THURSDAY 30 ★ Flexibility is key in tense relationships through the 31st

FRIDAY 31 ★

EYES ON THE DISTANT FUTURE

Don't underestimate the long-term impact of what occurs this month, for the stage is being set not only for the remainder of this year, but in fact for several years to come. Hardworking Saturn stands tensely opposed to surprising Uranus on **November 4,** a powerful aspect lasting through **July 2010.** It is likely you are already feeling on edge, itching to turn the most repressive parts of your life upside down and backward if necessary to gain your independence. Your frustration may not produce immediate results, but it offers clues to issues that must be resolved in the months and years ahead. It's likely that personal relationships will undergo major changes, dramatically affected by your current feelings of restlessness and an increasing need for freedom.

Fortunately, confident Jupiter relieves some of the tension this month as it harmonizes with the Saturn-Uranus opposition. Jupiter's third supportive sextile with Uranus on **November 13**—the first was on **March 28,** the second on **May 21**—allows you more latitude of self-expression as long as you respect the previously established rules and boundaries. Jupiter's easygoing trine with serious Saturn on **November 21** is the third in a series that began on **January 21** and was repeated on **September 8.** It reaffirms the changes you've made throughout the year based upon slow and steady growth. The Taurus Full Moon on **November 13** completes a practical Grand Earth Trine involving Jupiter and Saturn, yet imaginative Neptune's involvement suggests that you must rein in your illusions to manifest your dreams. The optimistic Sagittarius New Moon on **November 27** gives you great hope for the future and blesses you with the support of close friends and family.

SATURDAY 1

SUNDAY 2

MONDAY 3 ★ Stress won't disappear without effort through the 4th

TUESDAY 4 ★

WEDNESDAY 5

THURSDAY 6

FRIDAY 7

SATURDAY 8

SUNDAY 9

MONDAY 10 ★ **SUPER NOVA DAYS** Overcome your fears through the 13th

TUESDAY 11 ★

WEDNESDAY 12 ★

THURSDAY 13 ★

FRIDAY 14

SATURDAY 15

SUNDAY 16 ★ The sky's the limit if you embrace unconventional thoughts

MONDAY 17

TUESDAY 18

WEDNESDAY 19

THURSDAY 20

FRIDAY 21

SATURDAY 22

SUNDAY 23 ★ Leave the real world behind and partake in theoretical discussions

MONDAY 24

TUESDAY 25

WEDNESDAY 26

THURSDAY 27

FRIDAY 28 ★ You find a sensible path to unconventional desires through the 29th

SATURDAY 29 ★

SUNDAY 30

STRESS MANAGEMENT

December begins with a wonderful conjunction between beautiful Venus and broad-minded Jupiter on **December 1** in the resourceful sign of Capricorn, allowing you to approach an investment—financial or emotional—with extra common sense. But the sweet pleasures of the Venus-Jupiter conjunction are not long lasting, for the Sun drives toward its annual conjunction with the warrior planet, Mars, on **December 5.** This alignment in well-intentioned Sagittarius can give you good reason to initiate actions that move you closer to your goals, but can also stir up trouble at home or in a relationship. Your communication may be a bit on edge, for Mercury's squares to unpredictable Uranus on **December 5** and to respectful Saturn on **December 6** make it difficult for you to lead a discussion to a logical conclusion. Instead, you uncharacteristically fire off thoughts before you think about their consequences and then a moment later hesitate to say what's on your mind because you are afraid it might be inappropriate.

The scattered Gemini Full Moon on **December 12** falls in your 10th House of Career, increasing the stresses you already feel about your job. This Full Moon is square Saturn and Uranus, demonstrating the tenuousness of your hard-earned stability in life. Your originality sparkles as you participate in exciting discussions about unconventional ideas on **December 24,** supported by mental Mercury's sextile to Uranus the Awakener. Mercury's harmonious trine to Saturn on **December 26** helps you settle the energy and ground your erratic thoughts. The well-behaved Capricorn New Moon on **December 27** falls in your 5th House of Fun and Games, so be sure to fill up your calendar with holiday festivities.

MONDAY 1 ★ Make time for fun even if there's work to finish

TUESDAY 2

WEDNESDAY 3

THURSDAY 4

FRIDAY 5

SATURDAY 6

SUNDAY 7

MONDAY 8

TUESDAY 9

WEDNESDAY 10 ★ **SUPER NOVA DAYS** Clear the air through the 12th and move on

THURSDAY 11 ★

FRIDAY 12 ★

SATURDAY 13

SUNDAY 14

MONDAY 15 ★ A positive attitude and sincere effort will bring relief

TUESDAY 16

WEDNESDAY 17

THURSDAY 18

FRIDAY 19

SATURDAY 20

SUNDAY 21 ★ Shine a light on your fears through the 22nd

MONDAY 22 ★

TUESDAY 23

WEDNESDAY 24

THURSDAY 25

FRIDAY 26

SATURDAY 27 ★ Set your goals for next year and resolve to succeed

SUNDAY 28 ★

MONDAY 29 ★

TUESDAY 30 ★

WEDNESDAY 31 ★

2009 HOROSCOPE

VIRGO

AUGUST 23–SEPTEMBER 22

OVERVIEW OF THE YEAR

The patterns you establish and the choices you make this year will have an enduring impact on your life. Saturn, the planet of form and structure, remains in efficient Virgo until October 29—returning for a brief encore in 2010 before taking up a two-year residence in Libra. The presence of this crystallizing planet in your sign represents constraint, but it's not designed to bind you to your present circumstances. Its purpose is instead to help you recognize the relationship between your current limits and your future potential. While it can be discouraging to face the hard, cold reality of situations that have not lived up to your expectations, seeing exactly where you stand is a powerful position from which to make positive change. Saturn helps you define your goals, solidify plans, and apply the discipline and commitment required to make them work. **Don't allow self-doubt to deter you from reaching for the stars; you need only advance one careful step at a time to succeed.**

Unconventional individuals and impulsive partners bring surprises when revolutionary Uranus in emotional Pisces opposes Saturn on February 5 and September 15. This is part of a long series of destabilizing aspects between the planets of change and resistance that began late last year and ends next summer. Overcome a tendency to try to maintain the status quo, especially in relationships, because rigidity will only increase tension, perhaps leading to an explosion. **The unusual ideas you are facing can be just what you need to break down your barriers to a happier and more exciting life.** Feed your growing ambitions from a spring of innovation that reveals new ways to solve old problems. Balance stern Saturn's need for control with shocking Uranus's promise of discovery by maintaining flexibility in the face of the unexpected.

Expansive Jupiter in inventive Aquarius highlights your 6th House of Health, Work, and Daily Routines this year, broadening your perspective in these important areas. However, a Solar Eclipse on January 26 and a Lunar Eclipse on August 5 in Aquarius fall in the 6th House, indicating that you need to let go of some old ways before filling up on new ones. You're generally careful about making alterations in your life, but the natural effusiveness of Jupiter is increased by its conjunctions to idealistic Neptune on May 27, July 10, and December 21. Their union could float you on clouds of hope that overcome your practical nature, leaving you with inspiration but no ground in which to nurture its growth. You might find yourself swinging between extremes of optimism and despair—clearly not the best way to go. Don't allow cynicism to darken the essence of your ideals or dissuade you from aspiring to the highest levels of delight. **Temper your hopes with just a smidge of realism to ensure that they don't disappear in a puff of smoke** but become a long-lasting template for a more fulfilling future.

YOU'RE NUMBER ONE

Make yourself the top priority in relationships this year: Responsible Saturn in your 1st House of Self through October 29 puts the focus on your needs, desires, and well-being. Rather than making service to others the keystone of partnerships, pull back to a place of greater self-interest; this will give you the time, energy, and inclination to maximize your own strengths. Loving Venus goes retrograde in your 8th House of Intimacy on March 6 and turns direct in your 7th House of Partnerships on April 17—a period to reevaluate and, perhaps, alter your expectations of relationship and your commitments to others. If you're not satisfied with what you have, renegotiations are appropriate. A Capricorn Lunar Eclipse in your 5th House of Romance on July 7 is another potential turning point in matters of the heart, showing you that a current plan isn't working or that the burdens of responsibility you're carrying are too heavy. Don't be afraid to change course if you aren't headed in the right direction.

ON THE CUTTING EDGE

Trying different tasks at work or developing a brand-new set of skills can bring magic to your job this year. A superconjunction in Aquarius with visionary Jupiter, imaginative Neptune, and healing Chiron occurs in your 6th House of Employment, combining high tech, community service, and idealism on the job. Putting yourself on the cutting edge in your field will be more fun and fulfilling than playing it safe by sticking to what you already know. The retrograde periods of Mercury, ruler of your 10th House of Career, are times when minor complications and miscommunications can turn into major problems. Use these four critical periods—starting on January 11, May 6, September 6, and December 26—to backtrack and complete unfinished tasks, rebuild professional relationships, and tighten up your schedule to increase your efficiency.

CAREFUL REASSESSMENT

Investments, loans, and shared finances are due for a significant review this year when money-conscious Venus turns retrograde on March 6. The planetary ruler of your 2nd House of Income will travel backward in your 8th House of Joint Holdings until April 17. Backing out of existing deals to cut your losses or delaying new investments is wiser than forging ahead during this period. Enthusiastic Jupiter joins entrepreneurial Mars on February 17, stirring interest in a business opportunity. Yet Venus's pending retrograde and Mars's conjunction with illusory Neptune on March 8 turn yellow caution flags into red stoplights. Additionally, pay careful attention to the fine print when dealing with financial matters September 6–19, when messenger Mercury travels retrograde in your 2nd House of Money.

LET'S GET METAPHYSICAL

You tend to know more about diet and health than most people, yet your interests in these areas could be even stronger this year. Serious Saturn in your 1st House of Physicality instructs you to change habits to increase your level of fitness. However, oppositions to this otherwise stable planet from eccentric Uranus on February 5 and September 15 may produce sudden swings in your energy level. Exploring unconventional ways to attain optimal performance and vitality become especially appealing with "hungry to learn" Jupiter in your 6th House of Health. Its ongoing conjunctions with mystical Neptune and Chiron entice you to explore more subtle forms of healing.

PEACE AND UNDERSTANDING

Wisdom, faith, and inspiration enter your household this year, enlarging your perspective on family matters. Joyous Jupiter, the ruler of your 4th House of Home and Family, sails through progressive Aquarius in the company of Chiron and Neptune, allowing you to view your domestic situation in a more global manner. It's easier to let go of old grievances and negative patterns as hope is fueled by a vision of potentials—especially around May 23–27 and throughout December, when Jupiter, Chiron, and Neptune conjoin. Modernizing your living space or moving to a place with less restrictive values is possible now.

MARK YOUR CALENDAR

An Aquarius Lunar Eclipse on January 26 may trigger frustration on the road or an unexpected turn in academic matters. Venus, the ruler of your 9th House of Travel and Higher Education, is joined with erratic Uranus and opposed by Saturn during this important event. Stern Saturn forms a demanding square with Venus during the Cancer Solar Eclipse of July 21, which can also signal delays. Being flexible at these times helps you find alternative routes that allow you to reach your destination with less stress. Travel for pleasure when Venus opposes Jupiter on September 11. Schedule an important business trip around October 13 when Venus and Saturn connect in your sign while receiving organizational help from assertive Mars.

FINDING SPIRIT IN MATTER

Spirituality comes down to earth as part of your daily existence this year, illuminating the meaning of life through ordinary events. The metaphysically rich trio of Jupiter, Neptune, and Chiron transit your 6th House of Work and Service, elevating the significance of routine events and infusing you with hope and a sense of purpose on the job. The magic can strike you even while doing mundane chores, showing that you don't require an external authority or a special teacher to learn the most important lessons. A Leo Lunar Eclipse in your 12th House of Soul Consciousness on February 9 is charged up by electric Uranus, producing an epiphany that helps you let go of unnecessary psychological baggage.

RICK & JEFF'S TIP FOR THE YEAR
Stumbling to Success

The ongoing push-pull dynamic between your attraction to the new and your unwillingness to let go of the past is your theme this year. It may not be easy to find graceful ways to shift between these contrasting urges. Allow yourself to stumble awkwardly, if that's what it takes, rather than waiting for the perfect moment to change gears. Periods of transition and exploration of new territory are times when substance is more important than style. Permit yourself to be a beginner who makes mistakes in the process of learning, rather than having to be a pro who must master every move.

JANUARY

BACKING INTO THE FUTURE

Your ability to adapt to fluctuating conditions
is tested this month as Mercury, your ruling
planet, takes your mind on a wild journey. It
starts on **January 1** when the Messenger enters
quirky, airy Aquarius in your 6th House of Work
and Service. Alterations of routine can unravel
your well-crafted ways of managing daily life.
Unpredictable events or new procedures at your
place of employment can threaten efficient systems
that you understand thoroughly. Opportunistic
Jupiter's entry into Aquarius on **January 5** rein-
forces a trend of experimentation that requires
you to upgrade your skills and adjust your habits.
You can't fight progress, even if you're certain
that it's really a step backward. Help arrives on
January 10 with a tenacious Cancer Full Moon in
your 11th House of Groups that forms harmonious aspects to inventive Uranus and stable
Saturn, revealing a safe path between the future
and the past.

Mercury turns retrograde on **January 11**, beginning its three-week period of backtracking that so
often messes with communication, travel, and

technology. Be as patient as you can—this is a better time to reorganize and complete unfinished tasks than to start new projects. The progressive Aquarius New Moon on **January 26** is a Solar Eclipse conjoined by Jupiter that's likely to dramatize issues at work. Differences of opinion can grow into major battles—or you may simply be so bored or stressed that you're itching for change. Jupiter forms tense aspects to the slow-moving Saturn-Uranus opposition on **January 27–29** that emphasize the conflict between playing it safe and breaking free. It's a good time to broaden your perspective, but not yet the moment to act.

KEEP IN MIND THIS MONTH

You might not be able to keep all your ducks in a row, so lower your standards a little to keep your blood pressure down.

KEY DATES

★ **JANUARY 3-4**
the power of love
Kind Venus enters your 7th House of
Partnerships on **January 3**, attracting compassionate individuals who don't require you to be
perfect. Allow yourself the pleasure of sharing
time with someone who has no ambition other
than to enjoy you as you are. Venus aligns in
an easygoing sextile with potent Pluto on
January 4, enabling you to repair wounds and
take a relationship to a deeper level.

★ **JANUARY 11**
constructive self-reflection
Mercury turns retrograde, complicating life
with miscommunications for the next three
weeks that could have you heading one way
while a colleague is going off in another direction. Double-check conversations with teammates to avoid errors that waste time and
undermine trust. Reexamining your own methods can indicate where inefficiency slows you
down or limits the quality of your work. A

positive trine between the creative Sun and concrete Saturn gives you a solid center of self-awareness, allowing you to develop practical plans to achieve your long-range goals.

★ **JANUARY 18–21**
hold your tongue
Your mind stretches with bright ideas as Mercury joins broad-minded Jupiter on **January 18**. Absorbing so much information takes time, so don't expect to understand everything immediately. Your tendency to over-explain can add confusion when brevity would let you make your point. The Sun enters futuristic Aquarius on **January 19** and is conjoined by retrograde Mercury on **January 20**. Heightened mental activity can stress your nervous system, especially if you feel pressured to justify yourself. You may connect with critical information about yourself, but remember that you don't have to share it with others. Your need for privacy and verbal restraint is reinforced when Mercury backs into pragmatic Capricorn on **January 21**.

SUPER NOVA DAYS

★ **JANUARY 22–24**
pleasant surprises

Excitement stirs on **January 22**, when sociable Venus connects with experimental Uranus. Sudden shifts of mood can take you quickly from moments of delight to detachment and back again. Happily, active Mars aligns favorably with Uranus, giving you the agility to keep pace with these rapid changes. In fact, you should enjoy exploring new experiences that lighten your heart and open your eyes to different forms of fun. The planets fire in diverse directions on **January 24**, starting with a joyous aspect of hope and optimism between the Sun and jolly Jupiter. Mars is supported by responsible Saturn and sweet Venus to combine productivity with pleasure. However, Saturn also casts a shadow of self-doubt that can deflate delight with feelings of insecurity. Its goal, though, is not to stifle happiness, but to blend it with enough clarity and accountability to keep things real.

FEBRUARY

TESTING THE WATERS

Data, details, and communication slowly get back on track as your key planet, Mercury, shifts into forward gear on **February 1**. Its direct turn in your 6th House of Health, Work, and Daily Routines begins a settling-in period as you get more comfortable with new systems that you may have had difficulty grasping during the previous three weeks. Reliability in relationships of all kinds can be threatened by a powerful opposition between safe Saturn and unpredictable Uranus on **February 5**. This is the second in a series of five face-offs from your 1st House of Self to your 7th House of Others that's liable to keep partnerships on edge. You can reduce the pressure, however, if you focus on yourself and relax your expectations of a mate, colleague, or friend. New forms of alliances can emerge that give others more space to be themselves without the threat of a breakdown or breakup.

On **February 9**, a dramatic Leo Full Moon may spur you to let go of dreams that don't match your current reality. This Lunar Eclipse falls in your 12th House of Endings, reminding you that you don't have to hold on to every fantasy or try to be a hero for causes you've outgrown. Withdrawing from an exhausting struggle is not a surrender to outside forces, but a victory for your own well-being. Relationships return to the foreground when the Sun enters Pisces and your 7th House of Partnerships for a monthlong stay on **February 18**. The sensitive Pisces New Moon on **February 24** attracts charismatic individuals who encourage you to express your feelings more openly, which is bound to warm individual relationships and enhance your intuitive connection with others.

KEEP IN MIND THIS MONTH

No degree of preparation can keep surprises away. Adapting to the unexpected is much more effective than trying to suppress it.

KEY DATES

★ **FEBRUARY 1–2**
sugar and spice

The pace of life picks up with Mercury's forward turn on **February 1**, followed by Venus's entry into fiery Aries on **February 2**. The love planet in your 8th House of Deep Sharing sparks impulses that could shake up an intimate relationship. A sudden attraction or urge for new forms of fun with a current partner puts you in a risk-taking mood. Don't be shy about initiating change when you sense the need for more excitement.

SUPER NOVA DAYS

★ **FEBRUARY 4–5**
steep learning curve

Assertive Mars pops into conceptual Aquarius and your 6th House of Work on **February 4**, perhaps increasing tension on the job. New tasks or procedures require a period of adjustment, so don't expect a smooth transition immediately. The Saturn-Uranus opposition on **February 5** can tempt you to do something extreme, but there are brilliant solutions available that can produce change without disruption. You may feel underappreciated or manipulated as Venus, the Sun, and Pluto form difficult aspects with one another. Buried resentment may surface and undermine trust. If you focus on one issue at a time, however, you will discover resources to repair the damage.

★ **FEBRUARY 13–14**
mind games
Optimistic Jupiter joins with the karmic North Node of the Moon on **February 13**, attracting a wise teacher or helping you tap into your experience to guide others. Mental Mercury returns to intellectual Aquarius on **February 14**, adding a quirky twist to Valentine's Day. Talking is good, but if ideas become too abstract, the spirit of love can be lost.

★ **FEBRUARY 17–18**
with a little help from your friends
A high-powered conjunction between active Mars and Jupiter on **February 17** can light your passion for a project. If you want to make

it work in the long run, though, don't over-
reach right now. Assistance can come from an
unexpected source on **February 18** with a
sweet Venus-Mars sextile and the Sun's entry
into your 7th House of Partnerships. There
may be some complicated details to sort out
when Mercury's tense sesquisquare to Saturn
slows communication. Patient explanations
provide clarity to overcome obstacles.

★ **FEBRUARY 24–25**
too much information
Expect a wave of data and fresh ideas as fact-
filled Mercury joins visionary Jupiter on
February 24. You can make the strongest
impact by tempering your enthusiasm enough
to keep your feet solidly on the ground.
Streams of data from others may leave you
dizzy unless they slow down to show you how it
all can be applied. A harmonious hookup
between charming Venus and chatty Mercury
on **February 25** serves up sweet conversations
and boosts your self-esteem.

MARCH

CUT TO THE CHASE

Prepare to revisit relationship issues this month as Venus, the planet of love, turns retrograde in your 8th House of Intimacy on **March 6**. Reevaluating emotional and financial connections can stir up problems, but it's better to take the initiative than to sit back and react to what others do. The Full Moon in analytical Virgo in your 1st House of Self on **March 10** clearly puts the ball in your court. Stern Saturn's conjunction to the Moon shows the importance of discipline and self-control, especially in opposition to a potentially wild Sun-Uranus conjunction in your 7th House of Others. Even the most dependable allies may behave erratically and upset your plans. When you maintain personal authority, however, you're able to capture the sparks people ignite and use them to light a fire of inspiration for yourself. Assertive Mars entering vulnerable Pisces in your 7th House on **March 14** continues pushing buttons in relationships; be gentle if you'd like to turn conflict into the coziness that strengthens unions.

The Sun's entry into restless Aries on **March 20** marks the first day of spring and adds fire to your 8th House of Deep Sharing. Dramatic personal exchanges may threaten peace and harmony, but increase the likelihood of passion. Mental Mercury joins the scene on **March 25**, sharpening exchanges with quick comments and bright new ideas. Temper the tendency to tease, criticize, or respond to negative comments by others unless you're looking for a way out. The reckless Aries New Moon on **March 26** continues to flirt with the boundaries of partnerships. A hard square from compelling Pluto to this Sun-Moon conjunction could force a decision to make a definitive change, saving an alliance or finally ending it.

KEEP IN MIND THIS MONTH

There is no safety in standing still. Taking action, even if it seems risky, is the best way to keep your life on track.

KEY DATES

★ **MARCH 1**
sparring match
Chatty Mercury is sideswiped by a slippery
quincunx from Saturn early in the day, frustrating communication or unraveling plans.
Later, however, Mercury catches up with
hyperactive Mars to provoke fast talk and
aggressive conversation. Enjoy the mental
stimulation of a healthy debate or difference of
opinion, but back off if the need to be right
threatens to overrule love and kindness.

SUPER NOVA DAYS

★ **MARCH 8–10**
avoid assumptions
An idealistic but impractical Mars-Neptune conjunction on **March 8** can turn an act of charity
into an exhausting experience. Measure your
expenditures of time and energy carefully to
avoid wasting too much of either. Mercury
enters compassionate Pisces and your 7th
House of Partners, bringing sweet conversations
that can be misleading. Don't assume that

someone understands you because you share an emotional connection. An opposition between the Sun and rigid Saturn requires precision and a well-defined purpose to avoid irritation. A stressful semisquare from delicate Venus to Mercury tempts you to avoid speaking frankly and thus spare someone's feelings. Fortunately, a selective sextile between Mercury and Pluto on **March 10** will help you concentrate and find the right words to untangle any recent knots created by miscommunication.

★ **MARCH 18**
busy signal
Mercury's opposition to stifling Saturn can block or slow communication. If you aren't getting your message across, restate your point as clearly as you possibly can. If that doesn't work, don't despair, but wait for a better day to tell your story.

★ **MARCH 22–23**
shocking insights
A conjunction between Mercury and Uranus early on **March 22** tightens up your nervous

system and attracts unconventional ideas. Conversations can suddenly end or head off in strange directions. Keep an open mind, though, and a fresh perspective could give you a brilliant breakthrough. Expansion is awkward as Jupiter is challenged by Saturn and the Sun, preventing you from executing your big plans. An unrealistic Venus-Neptune semisquare may blur your financial or emotional judgment. You could have a moment or two of bliss, but a tough square between the Sun and purging Pluto on **March 23** is meant to help you cut through superfluous dreams and get you to the bottom line.

★ **MARCH 27–28**
soften your approach
Your bright ideas are hard to sell when speedy Mercury in Aries is snagged by challenging aspects from over-the-top Jupiter and hard-to-please Pluto on **March 27**. Calm your emotions to express your ideas with controlled passion, and you may be able to win over a demanding audience. Communication should be much easier on **March 28** when Mercury joins accommodating Venus, putting others in a more receptive mood.

APRIL

INVEST IN YOURSELF

Standing up for yourself is essential on **April 4** as assertive Mars in your 7th House of Others opposes Saturn in your 1st House of Self. Set clear boundaries with those who are unwilling to be cooperative, and state your expectations precisely. You are establishing a pattern in relationships that will work best when you know exactly what you want and aren't afraid to express it. The Full Moon in cooperative Libra on **April 9** falls in your 2nd House of Personal Resources, giving opportunities to increase your income and enhance your self-worth. A supportive trine to the Moon from generous Jupiter suggests that upgrading your work skills could lead to a raise. Clever Mercury's entry into earthy Taurus, also on **April 9**, grounds your thinking in practical terms and tempts you with the rewards of travel and additional education.

Romantic Venus stops her retrograde movement and shifts into direct motion on **April 17**. This may not produce an immediate impact on your love life, but it does initiate a process of moving forward in matters of the heart that may have recently been on hold. Consider renegotiating the terms of a personal or professional relationship if you're not happy. The Sun enters determined Taurus and your 9th House of Travel and Higher Education on **April 19**, a positive signal for widening your mental and physical horizons. Using the common sense of Taurus should help you find the most economical ways to explore your options. The practical Taurus New Moon on **April 24** is favored by a creative trine from regenerative Pluto. This potent heavenly body might help you resurrect an abandoned project and promote your beliefs with passion and power.

KEEP IN MIND THIS MONTH

Your distant goals can become attainable when they are rooted in realism, nourished with careful planning, and approached with patience.

KEY DATES

SUPER NOVA DAYS

★ **APRIL 2–4**
high-wire act
Information may not flow easily on **April 2**,
when verbal Mercury forms an awkward quincunx with grumpy Saturn. Avoid spending too
much time on details that you can address
later. A tense square between supersensitive
Venus and "tough as nails" Pluto on **April 3**
makes minor comments feel like major criticism. Instead of taking offense, investigate
what is being expressed. Tension remains on
April 4 with a stressful Mars-Saturn opposition that leaves little room for mistakes or
ambiguity. However, a smart sextile between
Mercury and Jupiter provides a perspective
that helps you make adjustments to your
course or skillfully explain your behavior.

★ **APRIL 9–11**
communication complexity
Expect a serious turn of mind on **April 9**, when
your planet Mercury enters steady Taurus and

forms a demanding sesquisquare with "straight shooting" Saturn. Stick to facts and avoid locking down in a protracted debate where stubbornness overrides common sense. An optimistic Sun-Jupiter sextile on **April 10** generates a more relaxed atmosphere in which you are not held accountable for every little thing you say or do. Deep thinking and powerful conversations flow naturally with a harmonious trine between Mercury and Pluto on **April 11**, making it possible to discuss delicate issues without wounding anyone.

★ **APRIL 13–15**
spontaneous combustion
Mercury aspects impatient Mars and eccentric Uranus on **April 13–14**, spurring weird conversations, verbal explosions, or brilliant breakthroughs. Mars and Uranus join on **April 15**, fomenting a rebellion in your 7th House of Partnerships that can shake up existing relationships or find you recklessly leaping into the arms of someone new. Experiment and have some fun when you feel safe enough to play.

★ **APRIL 22**
itching for action

Assertive Mars enters feisty Aries and is ready to rumble. A volatile square between Mercury and Jupiter leaves you prone to overstatement and can trigger an explosive difference of opinion. You hunger for adventure in your personal life or a chance to try something new in business. Don't stop these feelings; act on them with caution and sensitivity to turn a restless impulse into a lasting reward.

★ **APRIL 24–26**
twisted logic

Loving Venus returns to hot Aries and your 8th House of Intimacy on **April 24**, stoking your desires. If you're being pushed by someone else, however, don't make any quick decisions. Mercury's supportive sextile with electric Uranus suggests mental sharpness, yet its square with squishy Neptune on **April 25** can be a source of confusion. Mars forms a forceful square with Pluto on **April 26** that adds potency to everything you do, but makes it harder to change course if you go in the wrong direction.

MAY

EYE OF THE TIGER

Communication issues, especially in business matters, are key concerns this month with Mercury turning retrograde in your 10th House of Status on **May 7**. The speedy Messenger slipped into chatty Gemini on the last day of April, but its usual fast thinking and talking in the sign of the Twins are slowed by this backward turn. It's essential to avoid spreading yourself so thin with projects that you leave loose ends. Even your notorious attention to detail can waiver until Mercury rights its course and turns direct on **May 30**. The activities of outer planets are also critical this month as optimistic Jupiter joins compassionate Chiron on **May 23** and idealistic Neptune on **May 27** in your 6th House—the first in a series of super-conjunctions of this spiritually oriented trinity that recurs in **July** and **December**. This represents a wave of rising awareness of how you apply your energies in your daily life, opening the door to better health, opportunities to advance your skills, and more happiness on the job.

Complex personal issues may come to light on **May 9**, with the Full Moon in piercing Scorpio exposing secrets in your 3rd House of Communication. Intimate conversations can reveal uncomfortable facts as excessive Jupiter squares the Moon, but a higher level of emotional honesty is a worthwhile risk when you're seeking the truth. The New Moon in versatile Gemini on **May 24** plants so many seeds of possibility in your 10th House of Career, you may be overwhelmed with choices. Purging Pluto's cleansing quincunx to this Sun-Moon conjunction demands that you make your priorities clear and eliminate any inessential activities standing in the way of reaching your most compelling professional goals.

KEEP IN MIND THIS MONTH

You don't have to be great at everything to be successful. Concentrate your efforts on the most vital tasks, even if you must temporarily ignore other obligations.

KEY DATES

★ **MAY 5**
management material
The creative power of the Sun in resource-rich
Taurus in your 9th House of Big Ideas aligns
with concrete Saturn in your 1st House of
Physicality, paving the way to turning your
future hopes into your present reality. Impress
others now with your mature, competent, and
trustworthy approach.

★ **MAY 12–13**
starting over
Backpedaling Mercury forms an edgy semisquare with anxious Mars on **May 12**, increasing stress and inciting arguments. Breathe
slowly and deeply to gain clarity. Although your
perceptions are sharp, remaining calm is key
to being constructively creative instead of
reacting in negative ways. Mercury returns to
Taurus on **May 13**, which can prompt stubborn
thinking. Familiar ideas are appealing, even if
they are outmoded. When you return to basics,
make sure that it's more about finding a solid

foundation on which to stand than retreating from current reality.

SUPER NOVA DAYS

★ **MAY 16–18**
fearless flier
The Sun passes from a tense square with overconfident Jupiter to an integrating sextile with unorthodox Uranus on **May 16**, opening you to risky experiences that take you to the edge while also revealing new ways to find your way back to safety. Experimenting with unfamiliar activities is less dangerous than it seems, so push yourself a bit beyond your comfort zone. Stable Saturn turns direct in your sign, adding ballast to keep you grounded. However, feelings of vulnerability are possible on **May 17** with a dreamy Sun-Neptune square and a sensitive Mercury-Venus semisquare, undermining security and self-confidence. Retrograde Mercury joins the Sun on **May 18**, a great day for introspection to help you uncover a core issue, even if you aren't yet ready to explain it to others.

★ **MAY 20–21**

connect the dots

Ideas pop when the Sun enters airy Gemini and
Mercury squares Jupiter on **May 20**. Maintain
your credibility by avoiding information overload
and exaggeration. Mercury's smart sextile with
Uranus on **May 21** brings unexpected insights
that enable you to link individuals and synthe-
size data from diverse sources.

★ **MAY 30–31**

get off your soapbox

Communication begins to flow easily—allowing
you to be a more convincing spokesperson
for your beliefs—when Mercury turns forward
in your 9th House of Truth, Travel, and Higher
Education on **May 30**. Dynamic Mars pushes
into the 9th House on **May 31**, increasing your
desire to state your case, perhaps even to the
point of argument. Be especially cautious as
the warrior planet makes a sticky sesquisquare
with stern Saturn that can entrench you in a
long-term dispute. Focus on the facts to avoid
endless debate.

JUNE

UNEASY TEAMWORK

Managing your emotions is critical with the Full Moon in outgoing Sagittarius on **June 7**. The usual enthusiasm of this sign is constrained by a hard square from strict Saturn in Virgo as the demands of work and family can extend you to your limits. Setting boundaries may be exactly what you need. If you are overstretched with responsibilities, redefine your priorities and direct your resources appropriately. The Sun's presence in multifaceted Gemini in your 10th House of Career until **June 21** provides distractions that can scatter your forces. Your key planet, Mercury, enters Gemini on **June 13**, however, which can open your eyes to alternative ways to handle your job and also facilitate communication and connections that enhance your career. Visionary Jupiter turns retrograde in your 6th House of Work and Service on **June 15**, suggesting the value of retraining and refining your skills.

The Sun enters caring Cancer on **June 21**, marking the Summer Solstice in your 11th House of Groups and initiating a more dynamic period of teamwork and reliance on others. The importance of your relationships with pals and colleagues is underscored by the New Moon in gentle Cancer on **June 22**, which reveals challenges ahead. Potent Pluto's close opposition to the New Moon is associated with power struggles and, perhaps, a loss of trust with an associate. Aggressive Mars forms an edgy sesquisquare with Pluto on **June 23** to add more fire to an already tense situation. Fundamental differences regarding group goals and the best methods to achieve them may force you to back off from a project. It's better to recognize where your efforts won't be adequately rewarded than to spin your wheels with frustration.

KEEP IN MIND THIS MONTH

Putting others first can work for a while, but will wear you out if you continue to ignore your own needs to serve theirs.

KEY DATES

★ **JUNE 4-6**
use your influence

A powerful trine between active Mars and purging Pluto on **June 4** gives you the impetus to cut out unnecessary tasks and extraneous talk to operate at your highest level of efficiency. Your ability to motivate others is strong, too, since you know exactly what buttons to push to get the reactions you want. A stern Sun-Saturn square on **June 5** leaves no room for ambiguity, especially at work. Only take on responsibilities that are well defined and come with the authority you need to manage them properly. Vivacious Venus enters her sensual home sign of Taurus on **June 6**, sweetening your 9th House of Higher Thought and Faraway Places with images of spiritual comfort and island escapades.

★ **JUNE 9-10**
stuck inside a cloud

Brilliant ideas spurred by a sharp Mercury-Uranus sextile may be difficult to explain when followed by a fuzzy square from Neptune to Mercury on **June 9**. It takes imagination to describe your insights, which aren't easily translated into ordinary language. Making your point could be frustrating on **June 10**, when extravagant Jupiter squares detail-oriented Mercury. Overflowing words and data obscure the message. More is not necessarily better now, so don't be impressed by someone else's inflated promises—and avoid making any of your own.

SUPER NOVA DAYS

★ **JUNE 16–17**
something in the air
Mars and Uranus make a jumpy but innovative pair with their keyed-up semisquare on **June 16**. Spontaneity comes easily, but fast words and impulsive actions provoke unexpected responses. Experiments can produce amazing breakthroughs or blow up in your face, so be careful about where and how you take chances now. The Sun and Venus form tense aspects with rebellious Uranus on **June 17**, continuing to fill your life with electricity. Moods shift in

an instant and your inclination to compromise can disappear, creating conflict with authority figures. Happily, the Sun forms peaceful trines with forgiving Neptune and Jupiter, giving you the faith to find common ground.

★ **JUNE 21–23**
seeds of love
A sexy Venus-Mars conjunction on **June 21** jazzes up your Summer Solstice. This playful pair meets in your 9th House of Travel, raising your interest in exotic people and places. Harmonious trines from Venus and Mars to solid Saturn accompany the tender Cancer New Moon on **June 22**, turning creative ideas or romance into reality. However, Venus, the Sun, and Mars form tough aspects with "hard to please" Pluto on **June 23**, exposing gaps in a plan that will require cutbacks or additional resources. Resentment can rise with the pressure; dig deeper within yourself for answers rather than blaming others.

JULY

SHAKE IT UP

Two eclipses this month could lead you to a significant shift involving kids, self-expression, or friends. A Lunar Eclipse in responsible Capricorn on **July 7** falls in your 5th House of Romance, Children, and Creativity and could alter your plans in these areas. Discipline may fail and rules may be broken as your steady progress is interrupted. Still, with karmic Saturn, Capricorn's ruling planet, forming a supportive trine to this Full Moon, a change of routine may be exactly what you need. Instead of rigidly sticking to a fixed program as a parent, lover, or artist, it may be time to let go of your old methods and establish new ones to advance your personal interests. The New Moon in cautious Cancer on **July 21** is a Solar Eclipse in your 11th House of Groups that reflects changing patterns in teamwork. Reorganization at your job or within a volunteer organization is possible. A dependable old friend may no longer be available to you—yet you'll be experiencing more than enough new activity to make up for any sense of loss. Unique Uranus's trine to this Sun-Moon conjunction represents the stimulation that

95

can come from new people or practices. Exploring fresh areas of interest or trying new tasks within the team should put some excitement back into your life.

Your level of inspiration rises with boundless Jupiter's conjunctions to spiritual Neptune and healing Chiron on **July 10 and July 22**, the second in a series of aspects that began in **May** and end in **December**. You may be motivated to offer your services to a worthy cause and refine skills that support those efforts.

KEEP IN MIND THIS MONTH

When you face a potential loss with a creative and confident spirit, you can transform a threatening situation into a golden opportunity.

KEY DATES

SUPER NOVA DAYS

★ **JULY 1–2**
crazy love

On **July 1**, a romantic but unrealistic Venus-Neptune square nurtures your dreams of fascinating places and people. Your imagination is overfed by mental Mercury's trines to Neptune and Jupiter and a square with surprising Uranus. Brilliant thinking and clever words can be used to justify almost anything, so maintain a dash of skepticism to keep yourself grounded. Sensual Venus squares indulgent Jupiter and sextiles Uranus on **July 2**, intensifying your desire for more attention and affection. Opening yourself up to different kinds of delight, however, is an excellent idea, as long as the price you pay isn't too high.

★ **JULY 11–13**
subjective speech

Your ability to multitask shines now as Mercury aligns in a well-organized sextile to serious Saturn while active Mars enters diverse Gemini on **July 11**. Following your instincts is likely to be more successful than sticking to a rigid plan. Mercury joins the Sun on **July 13**, helping you clarify your intentions. This conjunction in the sensitive water sign of Cancer also adds an emotional quality that tends to make all communication feel highly personal.

★ JULY 15–17
fix your focus
You can waste your time with confusing conversations and imprecise information on **July 15**, so double-check details to avoid going off on a wild goose chase. A clear picture emerges on **July 16** as a clever Mercury-Uranus trine promotes original thinking. Yet chatty Mercury's tender semisquare with Venus adds vulnerability to personal exchanges; only gentle words will prevent wounded feelings. Mercury strides into bold Leo on **July 17**, stimulating grand ideas that you must analyze thoroughly before you make them public.

★ **JULY 21–23**
believe in yourself
Moods are mixed on **July 21**, when a tense
square between needy Venus and withholding
Saturn forces you to work harder for approval
and perhaps doubt yourself. The Sun's entry
into fiery Leo on **July 22**, though, could enhance
your self-confidence no matter what others
say. Your mind can shoot off in new directions
with a nervous Mercury-Uranus sesquisquare
on **July 23**. Pressure to conform to someone
else's vision could surface with a Sun-Pluto
quincunx on **July 23**, suggesting that a powerful person doesn't appreciate your profound
insights. If you're not being heard, wait for a
more inviting moment to make your point.

★ **JULY 30–31**
not the doctor
Mercury's oppositions to Jupiter, Chiron, and
Neptune rouse your inner poet and compassion
for others. Excessive optimism, though, may
encourage you to take on more than you can
handle. If you're unwilling to say no, do your
best to delay any commitments until you can.

AUGUST

ANALYTICAL MIND

Your thinking grows sharper as intellectual Mercury enters discerning Virgo on **August 2**. The narrowing lens of perception helps you cut through complex issues to get at key points, increasing your efficiency and ability to influence others. Still, it's helpful to step back and widen your perspective occasionally to make sure that your precisely defined picture fits into the larger scheme of things. The Full Moon on **August 5** is a Lunar Eclipse in unconventional Aquarius that falls in your 6th House of Health, Work, and Daily Routines, reminding you that new ideas and systems aren't always better than old ones. Fortunately, active Mars in flexible Gemini trines the Moon to show you how to make adjustments without making waves.

Finding balance between tomorrow's potential and today's reality can seem challenging with a clumsy quincunx between positive Jupiter and pragmatic Saturn on **August 19**. This second in a series of three aspects—which began on **March 22** and finishes on **February 5, 2010**—requires you to play the role of a skeptic to overly enthusiastic believers as well as act as a source of inspiration for those stuck in doubt and fear. Connecting with your inner guides and having faith in your vision of a brighter future are possibilities with the New Moon in expressive Leo on **August 20**. This energizing event occurs in your 12th House of Privacy, where its flames of creativity may be hidden from view. Nourish your hopes quietly instead of sharing them too soon. The Sun's entry into hardworking Virgo on **August 22** will put some wind into your sails. This solar energy in your sign increases confidence and vitality to enrich your personal life and empower you in business.

KEEP IN MIND THIS MONTH

It's very easy to spot errors, but you must also know how and when to point them out if you hope to make a positive contribution.

KEY DATES

★ **AUGUST 1–3**
after the deluge
An opposition between nurturing Venus in
Cancer and manipulative Pluto on **August 1**
agitates strong emotions. Speak honestly about
your feelings, but leave room for responses
from others. If all you're doing is venting, you
are more likely to drive someone away than get
satisfaction. Mercury's entry into Virgo on
August 2 leans toward logic. The communication planet's harmonious trine to Pluto on
August 3 helps you discuss difficult issues
effectively and repair any recent damage.

★ **AUGUST 10**
slow down
You may be feeling stressed at work as Mars in
your 10th House of Career pushes toward a
hard square with stringent Saturn. An aggressive boss or an overload of responsibilities
weighs heavily on your shoulders. Concentrate
on one task at a time—remember, going too
fast may lead to mistakes. Be gentle with

colleagues for whom a little nudge feels like a major shove.

★ **AUGUST 13–14**
all systems go
An enormous release of energy is possible as dynamic Mars aligns in a friction-free trine with upbeat Jupiter on **August 13**. This powerful pair connects work-related houses, giving you enthusiasm for new projects. The Sun's opposition to Jupiter on **August 14** lifts the wave even higher, nourishing your creativity with confidence. Fortunately, your instinctive sense of practicality should keep you from overstating your case or promising more than you can deliver.

SUPER NOVA DAYS

★ **AUGUST 17–18**
mixed signals
You can switch gears to match the moods of different colleagues and friends on **August 17**, for planets are firing off in several directions throughout the day. A sassy Sun-Mars sextile gets you support from unexpected sources, but mental Mercury and sober Saturn join up to

demand concentration, leaving little margin for error. Nevertheless, a spacey Sun-Neptune opposition and unstable Mercury-Jupiter quincunx keep providing opportunities for confusion. Trust your intuition—a Mars-Neptune trine can guide your actions more effectively than planning out every move. Expect surprises at work on **August 18**, when Mars in your 10th House forms a volatile square with Uranus. Instead of blowing up at someone or running for the hills, use this high-frequency force to invent new ways to get a job done.

★ **AUGUST 25–26**
hard to swallow
Anger and impatience could be ignited by a pushy Mercury-Mars square on **August 25**, just as Mars enters protective Cancer and Mercury enters polite Libra. A mild disagreement might grow into a serious conflict the next day, when both planets make hard aspects with passionate Pluto. If you can stay calm, however, the depth of your thinking and precision of your words could produce lasting breakthroughs of awareness and understanding.

SEPTEMBER

RELATIONSHIPS IN THE BALANCE

Examining relationships to adjust the balance between healthy self-interest and loving concern for others is a major theme for you this month. The Full Moon in psychic Pisces on **September 4** occurs in your 7th House of Partnerships, shedding new light on the subject. This compassionate water sign can wear down your self-restraint and open the way to richer emotional connections. Remember, however, that losing yourself in a co-dependent connection is not a recipe for long-term success.

Objective thinking is challenged when Mercury the Messenger turns retrograde on **September 7**. Your orderly world can be skewed by miscommunication and difficulty with details until your ruling planet turns direct again on **September 29**. Its backward turn starts in Libra in your 2nd House of Resources, indicating a potential review of your financial situation. On **September 17**, Mercury returns to your sign, making you more conscious of your appearance and attitude. Your flaws may seem more serious than is really the case, so even minor changes will have greater impact than you imagine.

The ongoing planetary tug-of-war between strict Saturn and rebellious Uranus flares up on **September 15** when they oppose each other again. This long series of aspects falls in your 1st House of Self and 7th House of Others, putting a strain on relationships. The New Moon in fussy Virgo on **September 18** triggers both planets as it joins Saturn and opposes Uranus, making you itchy for change—or desperate to stay put while a partner or close ally is anxious to make a move. Attractive Venus enters Virgo on **September 20**, swinging the balance in your favor by helping you recognize your true worth. The Sun enters coop-erative Libra on **September 22**, marking the Autumnal Equinox and illuminating gifts of beauty and harmony in your 2nd House of Resources.

KEEP IN MIND THIS MONTH

You don't always have to be consistent to have integrity. Changing your mind is healthier than maintaining a position that no longer feels right.

KEY DATES

★ **SEPTEMBER 3-4**
not ready to make nice
Words pack an extra punch when Mercury squares pugnacious Mars on **September 3**. If you can't resolve a difference of opinion quickly, it's best to back off—Mercury is almost standing still just four days prior to turning retrograde. Any agreements you make now are likely to need renegotiation later. Interpersonal dynamics can take on an edgy tone on **September 4** with a shaky sesquisquare between Venus and Uranus. Unexpected changes in your social life or a relationship are best met with a flexible attitude, because trying to control the situation or denying your feelings only increases tension.

★ **SEPTEMBER 11-12**
tunnel of love
Big waves are moving below the surface as powerful Pluto turns direct on **September 11** in your 5th House of Self-Expression. The desires for romance, play, and participation in

the arts that have been stewing inside of you
may be ready to flourish. An emotionally
expressive opposition between loving Venus
and opulent Jupiter expands your appetite for
pleasure. Have fun, but be cautious about
overindulging yourself, overestimating someone, or spending more than your budget
allows. A delicate semisquare between
Mercury and Venus on **September 12**
increases your sensitivity about personal matters. This is useful for intimate conversations,
but tends to make any critical comments
sound harsher than intended.

★ **SEPTEMBER 17**
pressure cooker
This complex day is heated up by the Sun's
explosive opposition to Uranus and constrict-
ing conjunction with Saturn. You can feel the
pressure to hold your ground even when a part
of you might want to run away from everyone
and everything. It's best to take care of yourself and recognize that you cannot control
what others do. Mercury squares unforgiving
Pluto just before retrograding back into Virgo,

which suggests that saying less is better than
speaking out at this volatile time.

SUPER NOVA DAYS

★ **SEPTEMBER 20–23**
master the madness
You are especially clear in your thinking as
Mercury joins the Sun and feeling self-confi-
dent with Venus entering capable Virgo on
September 20. The love planet's easy trine
with intense Pluto helps you cut through relationship clutter to make your needs known.
The winds shift with a spicy but dicey Venus-
Mars semisquare on **September 21** that
attracts both flirting and fighting. Mercury
joins serious Saturn as the Sun enters Libra
on **September 22**, a combination that favors
careful deliberation over impulsive actions.
However, Mercury's opposition to spontaneous
Uranus and quincunx with imaginative
Neptune on **September 23** is more intuitive
and creative than concrete and careful. And
the Sun's tense square with Pluto demands
strength and self-control, especially if you're
confronted by an adversary.

OCTOBER

MINING FOR GOLD

Money matters steal the spotlight this month as
the New and Full Moons fall in your houses of
finance. The initiating Aries Full Moon occurs on
October 4, stimulating ideas about investments
and business partnerships in your 8th House of
Shared Resources. Take the lead in a current eco-
nomic union, or consider starting a new one.
Friends or colleagues should be good sources
of information about ways to get a greater return
on your time, money, and energy. The New Moon
in artistic Libra lands in your 2nd House of
Possessions on **October 18**, providing a more
objective picture of your financial situation. Saturn
enters Libra on **October 29** to crystallize material
issues during the next two years. Draw on the
undeveloped gifts you already have within you. You
have creative skills that can be honed with
patience and discipline to upgrade your sense of
self-worth—and perhaps your income as well.

Intelligent Mercury provides a sharp perspective
to values and resources when it enters your 2nd
House on **October 9**. You may tend toward indeci-
siveness with this thoughtful planet in the

consensus-seeking sign of Libra. Consulting with others who recognize your talent can give you a boost, but don't let someone else's negative opinion overrule your own best instincts. Auspicious Jupiter turns direct in your 6th House of Work on **October 12**, raising your hopes for more rewarding employment. If the vision of greater fulfillment on the job seems beyond your reach, don't give up. Your success will be a benefit to others. Once you take the next step, support is likely to come from unexpected sources.

KEEP IN MIND THIS MONTH

Leisure activities that bring you joy could be critical components in creating a positive environment that attracts what you desire most.

KEY DATES

★ **OCTOBER 1–4**
rapid response

Mercury, just out of retrograde, is moving so
slowly that it forms two sweet sextiles with
Mars, one on **October 1** and the other on
October 4. These compatible aspects align
intellect and action to increase your efficiency.
You could, however, misinterpret messages on
October 4, when cloudy planetary conditions
make for a mixed forecast that blurs your
judgment. An electrifying Mercury-Uranus
square accelerates your mind into hyperdrive
to catch brilliant ideas . . . or maybe blow a
fuse. Fortunately, protective Mars in Cancer
creates an ingenious trine with fast-acting
Uranus to help you make rapid adjustments if
you veer too far off course.

SUPER NOVA DAYS

★ **OCTOBER 8–10**
controlled indulgence

Hone your concentration: A Mercury-Saturn
conjunction on **October 8** favors precision and

leaves little room for error. If you feel down or doubtful, excitement should arrive soon with a lively Venus-Uranus opposition on **October 9**. Celebrate a sense of freedom by exploring new delights. Logical Mercury returns to reasonable Libra late in the day, enabling you to see another point of view and to let go of old grievances. A sociable Sun-Jupiter trine on **October 10** blends work and pleasure in a most rewarding way. Use the Mercury-Pluto square to challenge your thinking instead of closing down in fear.

★ **OCTOBER 14–16**
building a mystery
The innocent romance of Venus entering lovely Libra on **October 14** is darkened by her square to controlling Pluto on **October 15**. Mistrust can be fed by confusion from Neptune's blur-ring square with Mercury. The current situa-tion is only a trigger for an old issue, so don't take it personally. A spiritual Sun-Neptune trine on **October 16** brings you the grace and clarity to feel pain without suffering from it, and to use that intuitive awareness to change your life.

★ **OCTOBER 20**
smooth operator

A divine trine between Mercury and Jupiter sweetly expands your mind. You can see how the smallest of facts are still part of a bigger picture. Life makes more sense. You deliver information effectively on the job or in any practical situation, combining logic with cleverness to find the easiest way to get around.

★ **OCTOBER 28–29**
watching the detective

Your perceptions are especially keen on **October 28** when Mercury enters intense Scorpio in your 3rd House of Information and contacts penetrating Pluto. You can see through others' stories and work your way to the truth. Secrets may be exposed in intimate conversations. Joy and generosity are present, too, with a big fat Venus-Jupiter trine promising a really good time. Nevertheless, a combative Mars-Sun square on **October 29** can make you fight for what you thought was already yours.

NOVEMBER

STUDENT OF LIFE

Travel and education are key this month. The earthy Taurus Full Moon on **November 2** falls in your 9th House of Higher Thought and Faraway Places, inspiring you to seek peace in a belief system or comfort in a distant land. You need a break from the pressures of your regular routine. Whether you plan a trip to the Caribbean, take a meditation class, or schedule a daily iPod moment to tune out the world, be sure to create space for yourself. Assertive Mars in your 12th House of Privacy squares this Sun-Moon opposition, telling you that you may have to struggle to get what you want, so don't be timid in pursuit of your dreams. Your ruling planet, Mercury, enters restless Sagittarius in your 4th House of Roots on **November 15**. An urge to know the truth about your family and its past evokes questions that require honest answers. Blunt statements can clear away cobwebs of confusion at home, but could also drive others away if too abrasive.

The New Moon in passionate Scorpio on **November 16** falls in your 3rd House of Information and Education. Its message is that you need to learn more and communicate with greater force. The intensity of this lunation is amplified by a powerful Saturn-Pluto square on **November 15** that will return on **January 31, 2010**, and **August 21, 2010**. Both planets demand that you concentrate to avoid feeling overwhelmed by circumstances beyond your control. Eliminate distractions, dig in and do research to find key ideas, and apply what you discover with precision. The Sun's entry into adventuresome Sagittarius on **November 21** stokes the fire in your belly, encouraging you to step out of your comfort zone and aim higher in your life.

KEEP IN MIND THIS MONTH

Moving gracefully from intense engagement to cool detachment allows you to play hard without wearing out your welcome or burning yourself out.

KEY DATES

★ **NOVEMBER 1–2**
high-speed connection

Mercury, in your 3rd House of Information, forms a sharp-edged square with aggressive Mars on **November 1** to rouse lively debate and instigate arguments. Expect aggravation when Mercury and Mars create irritable sesquisquares with shockingly brilliant Uranus on **November 2**. Quick thinking overtakes caution as the sensual Taurus Full Moon raises emotional tides, leading to breakthroughs in awareness—or breakdowns in communication.

SUPER NOVA DAYS

★ **NOVEMBER 5–8**
suspicious minds

Astute leadership skills originate from your clarity of purpose, empowered by a Mercury-Sun conjunction on **November 5**. However, a stubborn Mercury-Saturn semisquare on **November 6** requires you to express yourself more slowly to be understood by friends and colleagues. The plot thickens when Mercury semisquares Pluto on **November 7** as Venus enters skeptical Scorpio. Suspicion is difficult to avoid, even with your most trusted allies. Your personal values may be challenged, perhaps unfairly. Yet your exploration reveals what is most important to you. Cutting out unessential activities, objects, and individuals may feel harsh, but it's your key to satisfaction. Too much talk and an overabundance of data could have you seeking sanctuary in a quiet place on **November 8**.

★ **NOVEMBER 11**
this magic moment
A highly intelligent Mercury-Uranus trine supplies fresh insights and unconventional ideas. But apply them quickly, because an indefinite Mercury-Neptune square follows, making it easy to get distracted and lose track of the brilliant solutions you just discovered.

★ **NOVEMBER 21**
take it easy
Romance could get rocky with loving Venus caught up in the unrelenting pressure of the

Saturn-Pluto square. You feel the weight of the world on your shoulders, which can put the squeeze on relationships and up the cost of having a good time. Letting go of a plan that grows too complicated will reduce stress. Make this a no-frills day in which you can enjoy life's simple pleasures, relax, and recharge your batteries.

★ **NOVEMBER 29–30**
odds in your favor
Expressing yourself skillfully is simple with a Mercury-Jupiter sextile on **November 29**. This super-smart connection between two mental planets makes it easy to absorb new ideas and information. Big concepts crystallize, and you recognize useful ways to apply them in your daily life. You share your knowledge effectively thanks to a well-organized presentation. The tone is quite different on **November 30** when Mercury crosses paths with bright but eccentric Uranus. Their tense square can put you on edge and provoke impulsive speech, yet stepping outside your usual mental box can provide flashes of genius that solve problems in unexpected ways.

DECEMBER

SURPRISE ENDING

You must regroup, adjust your plans, and reorganize your life, for this transitional month features two Full Moons (one of them an eclipse), retrograde turns by Mars and Mercury, and the last of Jupiter's three magical conjunctions with Neptune and Chiron. On **December 2**, the Full Moon in verbal Gemini lights up your 10th House of Career, strengthening your communication skills and helping you make new connections. The danger of overextending yourself is reduced by steady Saturn's supportive trine to the Moon, enabling you to skillfully manage a busy schedule. Philosophical Jupiter joins healing Chiron on **December 7** and spiritual Neptune on **December 21** in the last of a series of conjunctions that began in May. This inspiring trio adds vision to your 6th House of Health and Daily Routines, lightening your present load with imagination and idealism and pointing the way to more fulfilling work in the future.

Domestic matters take the spotlight with a free-spirited Sagittarius New Moon in your 4th House of Roots on **December 16**. A tense square from erratic Uranus may create sudden chaos on the home front, but shaking the family tree unhooks you from old unhealthy patterns and opens the way to bigger dreams for tomorrow. Militant Mars starts marching backward in your 12th House of Secrets on **December 20**, energizing you with inner motivation well into next year. Turning anger into a creative plan is imperative if you hope to avoid resentment that could simmer dangerously for weeks. Mercury's retrograde shift on **December 26** ends the year on an introspective note. The moody Cancer Full Moon on **December 31** is a Lunar Eclipse in your 11th House of Groups that could lead to a parting of the ways with a colleague or friend.

KEEP IN MIND THIS MONTH

Keep your ambition and sense of duty in check to avoid overloading yourself with more responsibilities than you can comfortably handle.

KEY DATES

★ **DECEMBER 5–8**
breaking the silence

Serious thinking prevails as Mercury enters responsible Capricorn on **December 5**. This planet's presence in your 5th House of Self-Expression, however, suggests that you have something very important to say. Preparing for an important presentation, whether personal or professional, takes on additional urgency when Mercury joins relentless Pluto and squares demanding Saturn on **December 7**. Master your message to overcome inner doubt or external critics. Don't be intimidated into silence, even if it's difficult to speak what's on your mind. An edgy Mercury-Mars sesquisquare on **December 8** may spark confrontation, yet when you focus on facts, you can be very convincing.

★ **DECEMBER 10–11**
truth or dare

Enthusiasm allows you to be more open than usual due to a boundless Mercury-Jupiter semisquare on **December 10**. An energetic trine between the Sun and Mars could even dare you into revealing a secret. It's better to be frank and push some limits than to stifle communication. Besides, Mercury's semisquare with compassionate Neptune on **December 11** can bring either forgiveness—or so much confusion that whatever you say will be forgotten. The quality of feeling behind any idea is likely to have more impact than facts, so use your intuition to read between the lines and your emotions to send a compelling message.

★ **DECEMBER 19–21**
just out of reach
You could be feeling antsy with a restless square from Venus to electric Uranus on **December 19**. Expect last-minute changes of social plans or sudden shifts of mood. Aesthetic improvements in your home can scratch your itch for new sources of pleasure. The reticence of Mars retrograde on **December 20** contrasts with a joyful Venus-Jupiter sextile. Use caution to avoid expensive excesses. Jupiter's conjunction and Venus's sextile with

Neptune blankets **December 21** with clouds of hope and faith, reinforced by the Sun's entry into traditional Capricorn on the Winter Solstice. Mercury's quincunx with Mars stirs up disagreements that are best avoided—they can be difficult to resolve.

SUPER NOVA DAYS

★ **DECEMBER 24–27**
peaceful warrior
Power struggles are possible when the Sun joins provocative Pluto on **December 24** and squares unyielding Saturn on **December 25**. An aggressive Sun-Mars sesquisquare increases your likelihood of frustration. Mercury's backward turn on **December 26** can mix up messages, while a hard-nosed Mars-Saturn semisquare on **December 27** turns up the heat. Peace is especially desirable during the holidays, but if you must fight, be clear and concise. Make your point with strength and focus to keep conflict to a minimum. Victory is not about winning over the other person, but stating your position with well-controlled passion and precision.

APPENDIXES

★

2009 MONTH-AT-A-GLANCE ASTROCALENDAR

★

FAMOUS VIRGOS

★

VIRGO IN LOVE

THURSDAY 1

FRIDAY 2

SATURDAY 3 ★ The 4th enables you to repair wounds and take a relationship to a deeper level

SUNDAY 4 ★

MONDAY 5

TUESDAY 6

WEDNESDAY 7

THURSDAY 8

FRIDAY 9

SATURDAY 10

SUNDAY 11 ★ You develop practical plans to achieve your long-range goals

MONDAY 12

TUESDAY 13

WEDNESDAY 14

THURSDAY 15

FRIDAY 16

SATURDAY 17

SUNDAY 18 ★ Heightened mental activity can stress your nervous system

MONDAY 19 ★

TUESDAY 20 ★

WEDNESDAY 21 ★

THURSDAY 22 ★ **SUPER NOVA DAYS** Blend happiness with enough clarity and accountability to keep things real

FRIDAY 23 ★

SATURDAY 24 ★

SUNDAY 25

MONDAY 26

TUESDAY 27

WEDNESDAY 28

THURSDAY 29

FRIDAY 30

SATURDAY 31

SUNDAY 1 ★ Initiate change when you sense the need for more excitement

---

MONDAY 2 ★

TUESDAY 3

WEDNESDAY 4 ★ **SUPER NOVA DAYS** Buried resentment may surface and undermine trust

---

THURSDAY 5 ★

FRIDAY 6

SATURDAY 7

SUNDAY 8

MONDAY 9

TUESDAY 10

WEDNESDAY 11

THURSDAY 12

FRIDAY 13 ★ If ideas become too abstract, the spirit of love can be lost

---

SATURDAY 14 ★

SUNDAY 15

MONDAY 16

TUESDAY 17 ★ Patient explanations provide clarity to overcome obstacles

---

WEDNESDAY 18 ★

THURSDAY 19

FRIDAY 20

SATURDAY 21

SUNDAY 22

MONDAY 23

TUESDAY 24 ★ Temper your enthusiasm and make a strong impact

WEDNESDAY 25 ★

THURSDAY 26

FRIDAY 27

SATURDAY 28

SUNDAY 1 ★ Enjoy the stimulation of a healthy debate

MONDAY 2

TUESDAY 3

WEDNESDAY 4

THURSDAY 5

FRIDAY 6

SATURDAY 7

SUNDAY 8 ★ SUPER NOVA DAYS Measure your expenditures carefully

---

MONDAY 9 ★

TUESDAY 10 ★

WEDNESDAY 11

THURSDAY 12

FRIDAY 13

SATURDAY 14

SUNDAY 15

MONDAY 16

TUESDAY 17

WEDNESDAY 18 ★ Communication is blocked, state your point clearly

---

THURSDAY 19

FRIDAY 20

SATURDAY 21

SUNDAY 22 ★ A moment of bliss comes your way on the 23rd

MONDAY 23 ★

TUESDAY 24

WEDNESDAY 25

THURSDAY 26

FRIDAY 27 ★ Calm your emotions to express ideas with controlled passion

---

SATURDAY 28 ★

SUNDAY 29

MONDAY 30

TUESDAY 31

WEDNESDAY 1

THURSDAY 2 ★ **SUPER NOVA DAYS** Make quick adjustments to correct your skillfully planned course

FRIDAY 3 ★

SATURDAY 4 ★

SUNDAY 5

MONDAY 6

TUESDAY 7

WEDNESDAY 8

THURSDAY 9 ★ Deep thinking and powerful conversations flow naturally

FRIDAY 10 ★

SATURDAY 11 ★

SUNDAY 12

MONDAY 13 ★ When it's safe enough to play, experiment and have fun!

TUESDAY 14 ★

WEDNESDAY 15 ★

THURSDAY 16

FRIDAY 17

SATURDAY 18

SUNDAY 19

MONDAY 20

TUESDAY 21

WEDNESDAY 22 ★ Hunger for adventure in your personal life is apparent

THURSDAY 23

FRIDAY 24 ★ Mental sharpness adds potency to everything you do

SATURDAY 25 ★

SUNDAY 26 ★

MONDAY 27

TUESDAY 28

WEDNESDAY 29

THURSDAY 30

FRIDAY 1

SATURDAY 2

SUNDAY 3

MONDAY 4

TUESDAY 5 ★ Impress others with your competent and trustworthy approach

WEDNESDAY 6

THURSDAY 7

FRIDAY 8

SATURDAY 9

SUNDAY 10

MONDAY 11

TUESDAY 12 ★ Remaining calm is key to being constructive

WEDNESDAY 13 ★

THURSDAY 14

FRIDAY 15

SATURDAY 16 ★ SUPER NOVA DAYS Solve a core issue through introspection

SUNDAY 17 ★

MONDAY 18 ★

TUESDAY 19

WEDNESDAY 20 ★ Avoid information overload and exaggeration

THURSDAY 21 ★

FRIDAY 22

SATURDAY 23

SUNDAY 24

MONDAY 25

TUESDAY 26

WEDNESDAY 27

THURSDAY 28

FRIDAY 29

SATURDAY 30 ★ Communication begins to flow easily

SUNDAY 31 ★

MONDAY 1
TUESDAY 2
WEDNESDAY 3
THURSDAY 4 ★ Operate at your highest level of efficiency on the 4th
FRIDAY 5 ★
SATURDAY 6 ★
SUNDAY 7
MONDAY 8
TUESDAY 9 ★ Avoid making inflated promises
WEDNESDAY 10 ★
THURSDAY 11
FRIDAY 12
SATURDAY 13
SUNDAY 14
MONDAY 15
TUESDAY 16 ★ **SUPER NOVA DAYS** Experiments can produce amazing breakthroughs
WEDNESDAY 17 ★
THURSDAY 18
FRIDAY 19
SATURDAY 20
SUNDAY 21 ★ Rather than blaming others, dig within yourself for answers
MONDAY 22 ★
TUESDAY 23 ★
WEDNESDAY 24
THURSDAY 25
FRIDAY 26
SATURDAY 27
SUNDAY 28
MONDAY 29
TUESDAY 30

WEDNESDAY 1 ★ SUPER NOVA DAYS Open up to different forms of delight

---

THURSDAY 2 ★

FRIDAY 3

SATURDAY 4

SUNDAY 5

MONDAY 6

TUESDAY 7

WEDNESDAY 8

THURSDAY 9

FRIDAY 10

SATURDAY 11 ★ Following your instincts on the 11th is highly successful

---

SUNDAY 12 ★

MONDAY 13 ★

TUESDAY 14

WEDNESDAY 15 ★ A clear picture emerges on the 16th stimulating grand ideas

---

THURSDAY 16 ★

FRIDAY 17 ★

SATURDAY 18

SUNDAY 19

MONDAY 20

TUESDAY 21 ★ Enhance your self-confidence on the 22nd

WEDNESDAY 22 ★

THURSDAY 23 ★

FRIDAY 24

SATURDAY 25

SUNDAY 26

MONDAY 27

TUESDAY 28

WEDNESDAY 29

THURSDAY 30 ★ Don't take on more than you can handle

FRIDAY 31 ★

SATURDAY 1 ★ Strong emotions are agitated on the 1st

SUNDAY 2 ★

MONDAY 3 ★

TUESDAY 4

WEDNESDAY 5

THURSDAY 6

FRIDAY 7

SATURDAY 8

SUNDAY 9

MONDAY 10 ★ Slow down—concentrate on one task at a time

TUESDAY 11

WEDNESDAY 12

THURSDAY 13 ★ Your creativity is nourished with confidence

FRIDAY 14 ★

SATURDAY 15

SUNDAY 16

MONDAY 17 ★ **SUPER NOVA DAYS** Support comes from unexpected sources

TUESDAY 18 ★

WEDNESDAY 19

THURSDAY 20

FRIDAY 21

SATURDAY 22

SUNDAY 23

MONDAY 24

TUESDAY 25 ★ Prepare for lasting breakthroughs of understanding

WEDNESDAY 26 ★

THURSDAY 27

FRIDAY 28

SATURDAY 29

SUNDAY 30

MONDAY 31

TUESDAY 1

WEDNESDAY 2

THURSDAY 3 ★ Controlling situations or denying feelings increases tension

FRIDAY 4 ★

SATURDAY 5

SUNDAY 6

MONDAY 7

TUESDAY 8

WEDNESDAY 9

THURSDAY 10

FRIDAY 11 ★ Act on your desires: romance, play, and creativity

SATURDAY 12 ★

SUNDAY 13

MONDAY 14

TUESDAY 15

WEDNESDAY 16

THURSDAY 17 ★ It's a volatile time—saying less is better

FRIDAY 18

SATURDAY 19

SUNDAY 20 ★ **SUPER NOVA DAYS** You are especially clear in your thinking on the 20th

MONDAY 21 ★

TUESDAY 22 ★

WEDNESDAY 23 ★

THURSDAY 24

FRIDAY 25

SATURDAY 26

SUNDAY 27

MONDAY 28

TUESDAY 29

WEDNESDAY 30

THURSDAY 1 ★ Brilliant ideas are electrified in your mind

FRIDAY 2 ★

SATURDAY 3 ★

SUNDAY 4 ★

MONDAY 5

TUESDAY 6

WEDNESDAY 7

THURSDAY 8 ★ **SUPER NOVA DAYS** Work and pleasure blend rewardingly

FRIDAY 9 ★

SATURDAY 10 ★

SUNDAY 11

MONDAY 12

TUESDAY 13

WEDNESDAY 14 ★ Use your intuitive awareness to change your life

THURSDAY 15 ★

FRIDAY 16 ★

SATURDAY 17

SUNDAY 18

MONDAY 19

TUESDAY 20 ★ You inform effectively on the job and in practical situations

WEDNESDAY 21

THURSDAY 22

FRIDAY 23

SATURDAY 24

SUNDAY 25

MONDAY 26

TUESDAY 27

WEDNESDAY 28 ★ Joy and generosity are present on the 29th

THURSDAY 29 ★

FRIDAY 30

SATURDAY 31

SUNDAY 1 ★ Emotional tides lead to breakthroughs in awareness

MONDAY 2 ★

TUESDAY 3

WEDNESDAY 4

THURSDAY 5 ★ SUPER NOVA DAYS Ideas about relationships, self-worth, and personal values are challenged

FRIDAY 6 ★

SATURDAY 7 ★

SUNDAY 8 ★

MONDAY 9

TUESDAY 10

WEDNESDAY 11 ★ Don't lose track of the brilliant solutions you just discovered

THURSDAY 12

FRIDAY 13

SATURDAY 14

SUNDAY 15

MONDAY 16

TUESDAY 17

WEDNESDAY 18

THURSDAY 19

FRIDAY 20

SATURDAY 21 ★ Letting go of a complicated plan will reduce stress

SUNDAY 22

MONDAY 23

TUESDAY 24

WEDNESDAY 25

THURSDAY 26

FRIDAY 27

SATURDAY 28

SUNDAY 29 ★ A flash of genius solves problems in unexpected ways

MONDAY 30 ★

TUESDAY 1	
WEDNESDAY 2	
THURSDAY 3	
FRIDAY 4	
SATURDAY 5 ★	Preparing for an important presentation takes on urgency on the 7th
SUNDAY 6 ★	
MONDAY 7 ★	
TUESDAY 8 ★	
WEDNESDAY 9	
THURSDAY 10 ★	Enthusiasm allows you to be more open than usual on the 10th
FRIDAY 11 ★	
SATURDAY 12	
SUNDAY 13	
MONDAY 14	
TUESDAY 15	
WEDNESDAY 16	
THURSDAY 17	
FRIDAY 18	
SATURDAY 19 ★	Use caution to avoid expensive excesses
SUNDAY 20 ★	
MONDAY 21 ★	
TUESDAY 22	
WEDNESDAY 23	
THURSDAY 24 ★	SUPER NOVA DAYS Power struggles are possible on the 24th
FRIDAY 25 ★	
SATURDAY 26 ★	
SUNDAY 27 ★	
MONDAY 28	
TUESDAY 29	
WEDNESDAY 30	
THURSDAY 31	

FAMOUS VIRGOS

River Phoenix	★	8/23/1970
Kobe Bryant	★	8/23/1978
Gene Kelly	★	8/23/1912
Dave Chappelle	★	8/24/1973
Regis Philbin	★	8/25/1933
Sean Connery	★	8/25/1930
Elvis Costello	★	8/25/1954
Claudia Schiffer	★	8/25/1970
Gene Simmons	★	8/25/1949
Mother Teresa	★	8/27/1910
Lyndon B. Johnson	★	8/27/1908
LeAnn Rimes	★	8/28/1982
Johann Wolfgang von Goethe	★	8/28/1749
Michael Jackson	★	8/29/1958
Ingrid Bergman	★	8/29/1915
Charlie Parker	★	8/29/1920
Clara Bow	★	8/29/1905
John McCain	★	8/29/1936
Preston Sturges	★	8/29/1898
Mary Wollstonecraft Shelley	★	8/30/1797
Andy Roddick	★	8/30/1982
Ted Williams	★	8/30/1918
Cameron Diaz	★	8/30/1972
Van Morrison	★	8/31/1945
Richard Gere	★	8/31/1949
Lily Tomlin	★	9/1/1939
Dr. Phil McGraw	★	9/1/1950
Rocky Marciano	★	9/1/1923
Keanu Reeves	★	9/2/1964
Lennox Lewis	★	9/2/1965
Salma Hayek	★	9/2/1966
Beyoncé Knowles	★	9/4/1981
Damon Wayans	★	9/4/1960
Mike Piazza	★	9/4/1968
Raquel Welch	★	9/5/1940

FAMOUS VIRGOS

Freddie Mercury	★	9/5/1946
Rosie Perez	★	9/6/1964
Buddy Holly	★	9/7/1936
Patsy Cline	★	9/8/1932
Peter Sellers	★	9/8/1925
Roger Waters	★	9/9/1943
Otis Redding	★	9/9/1941
Hugh Grant	★	9/9/1960
Arnold Palmer	★	9/10/1929
Randy Johnson	★	9/10/1963
D. H. Lawrence	★	9/11/1885
O. Henry	★	9/11/1862
Barry White	★	9/12/1944
Claudette Colbert	★	9/13/1903
Roald Dahl	★	9/13/1916
Agatha Christie	★	9/15/1890
Oliver Stone	★	9/15/1946
Prince Harry	★	9/15/1984
Lauren Bacall	★	9/16/1924
B. B. King	★	9/16/1925
Anne Bancroft	★	9/17/1931
Greta Garbo	★	9/18/1905
Frankie Avalon	★	9/18/1939
Lance Armstrong	★	9/18/1971
Trisha Yearwood	★	9/19/1964
Mama Cass Elliott	★	9/19/1941
Adam West	★	9/19/1928
Dr. Joyce Brothers	★	9/20/1928
Sophia Loren	★	9/20/1934
Upton Sinclair	★	9/20/1878
Bill Murray	★	9/21/1950
Faith Hill	★	9/21/1967
Stephen King	★	9/21/1947
H. G. Wells	★	9/21/1866
Joan Jett	★	9/22/1958
Andrea Bocelli	★	9/22/1958

VIRGO IN LOVE

VIRGO–ARIES (MARCH 21–APRIL 19)

Your personality is detail-oriented and analytical.
You're a perfectionist who likes things to be done
efficiently. You can be judgmental in ways that
become self-defeating if not kept under control.
Aries, however, lives a life that's somewhat looser.
The Ram is a pioneer who pushes ahead with less
organization and minimal emphasis on detail,
which can irritate you. You'll find yourself judging
irrepressible Aries as juvenile or simplistic, which
isn't necessarily accurate. In spite of your great
ability to focus on details, you can miss the bigger
picture in life's everyday dramas. If the Moon in your
chart is in a fire or air sign, you'll appreciate your
Aries lover's zest for life. If your Moon is in an earth
or water sign, you'll be more cautious to endorse
your Ram's sense of immediacy. The bottom line is
that Aries are movers and shakers—your life will
not be dull if you partner with a Ram. Your sense of
stability can help ground Aries, and you can make
good business partners. If you can learn to accept
your differences, you stand to learn much from
happy Aries who can, in turn, light up your life.

VIRGO–TAURUS (APRIL 20–MAY 20)

You and Taurus can make a great pair, for you find a real companion in the Bull, who complements your analytical style with common sense. You are both earth signs and can encourage productivity in each other, especially in the realm of business and practical matters concerning home and family. Your heightened sense of perfectionism blends very well with the artistic and sensual tastes of your Taurus lover. If, however, your Venus is in Leo or Libra, you may have ongoing disagreements about what you each consider tasteful. In Taurus, you find someone who can create an environment that is clean, well-organized, and simplistically beautiful. Your partner will probably pay attention to money—balancing your frugal ways with their abundant desires. Your nature-loving Taurus will most likely also enjoy camping and outdoor hikes, and if they do love the outdoors, they may actually incorporate natural, earthy themes into home décor, including lots of plants and a useful herb or vegetable garden. This is a down-to-earth, no-nonsense match that can survive the toughest of times and thrive for many happy years.

VIRGO–GEMINI (MAY 21–JUNE 20)

Both you and Gemini have the planet Mercury as your ruling planet. Mercury is associated with all forms of communication, so words, ideas, and conversations are lively and emphasized in this relationship. Since you both love a well-crafted sentence, together you can revel in the beauty of speech and music. With all these similarities, you might think this is a match made in heaven, but your styles of communication are quite different. Your refined style is practical and highly critical, making you a talented editor. Meanwhile, your Gemini mate is comfortable when talking without a script, making him or her more social and very charming at parties. If your Mars is in a fire or air sign, you may feel at ease jumping into Gemini's clever conversations. But if your Mars is in a water or earth sign, you may have difficulty keeping up. Wherever your Mars is, you may find it hard to relax around your restless Gemini lover. You can burn off some of this energy by engaging in discussions about books, participating together in literary projects, or exploring new forms of communication. Romantic involvement with you two rationalists is both physical *and* mental. The right words can inspire much passion.

VIRGO-CANCER (JUNE 21–JULY 22)

You are tactful, well-mannered, and have a high-strung nervous system. You find much comfort within the protective sphere of a Cancer mate. You are apt to set the foundation for the home on the material plane by organizing and tidying up the environment. Your Cancer lover will warm and soften your cool aesthetic tastes with photos of friends, cozy blankets on chairs, and emotionally nurturing family memorabilia. The two of you must find a balance, however, because your Crab is sentimental, and in holding onto the past, can create clutter. You prefer neat and clean spaces—except when it's your own clutter, which isn't a mess, just an organized pile. Although you bring a rational point of view to your partner, he or she may not be as impressed with facts and figures as you are. This makes you crazy, for emotionally driven Cancers are more concerned with their gut intuition, and all the logic in the world isn't going to change their minds. If, however, the Moon in your chart is in a water sign, you may acknowledge the supremacy of intuition over logic. Nonetheless, communication flows well between you two; you'll be able to create many fond memories.

VIRGO-LEO (JULY 23–AUGUST 22)

You are very strong within your own self, even if you present a timid appearance. As such, you are not apt to need outside encouragement on a daily basis. And, because you have a sharp mind, you can be self-critical to a fault. You have, however, an uncanny endurance that gets you through most obstacles. Your sharp mind is connected to your sharp eye, and as such you can be overly critical of others, too. This doesn't fly with your Leo mate. The Lion cannot easily take criticism and may be in need of ongoing praise and attention, displaying strengths in other areas, such as devotion, love, and generosity. Your quiet humility may cause you to bump heads with the prideful Lion, who needs outward displays of affection to strengthen self-confidence and courage. If your chart has the Moon, Mercury, or Venus in Leo, you will be able to assimilate these leonine traits, using candor and humor to get around the irritations you may feel. Your Leo lover can appreciate your razor-sharp wit, but whatever you do, don't tease him or her. Handle Lions with respect and honor, even when they are displaying childlike tendencies, and you can find yourself in a winner of a relationship.

VIRGO–VIRGO (AUGUST 23–SEPT. 22)

When others are in the company of two Virgos, they may feel as though they are witnessing an elite club meeting in progress. You Virgos can find delight in each another for many reasons. You both see yourselves as slightly superior to the rest of the human race due to your innate organizational skills, acute detail in work, and your ability to execute ideas and put them to productive use. You are amazing, no doubt! No detail is too small to tackle or explain. The target problem areas of the relationship develop when your fastidious minds compete as to which one of the two will rule the roost. You both have set and exacting ideas, but they may differ widely, especially if Mercury is in different signs in your individual charts. If, however, they are in the same sign, your ideas may be more complementary, balanced, and cooperative. This mutual and shared intellectual perspective will allow for peace and happiness. There is good wit and humor shared between you two, but it is usually on the dry side. This relationship may function well and have an efficient practicality, but it's probably not going to be very warm and fuzzy.

VIRGO-LIBRA (SEPT. 23-OCT. 22)

You are as reflective, analytical, and refined as your Libra lover and can get along famously, as long as Libra isn't too wishy-washy when it comes to making decisions. You'll probably get annoyed with the indecision of your partner, who would rather avoid picking one option over another. Libra will feel pressured by you, even if that's not your intention. Libra will feel judged under your critically discerning eye. But it's not just about making decisions. You may also be critical of his or her laziness. And, unless you have Mercury or Venus in Libra in your chart, you'll probably think your Libra mate isn't very practical ... and you'll be right! Libras are more interested in aesthetics than utility. Your Libra will want the walls painted white because it looks better, but you'll want them a light ivory because dirt won't show up as quickly. Actually, you are both keen on beauty and balance, and can build a lovely environment that others find refreshing, clean, and stimulating. Together, you can be prosperous and indulge in the finer things in life. With some individual adjustments, this can be a compatible relationship with good potential.

VIRGO–SCORPIO (OCT. 23-NOV. 21)

You appreciate tact, as well as a well-groomed environment. You dislike anything crude or unpolished, preferring to relate with people who will not offend or embarrass your sense of decency. Your Scorpio partner, although quiet and deeply honest, may at times step over the line of acceptability for your taste. Overtly blunt, and not afraid to venture deep into the mysterious dark edges of life, your passionate Scorpio mate is driven to plunge into experiences with unedited intensity. Let's face it: you are attracted to Scorpio's frank and honest personality, but you wish your mate could be emotionally more mellow. You will have to get past the manner in which your lover presents his or her views, or your refined nature may feel overwhelmed. Sometimes Scorpio's volcanic power actually scares you, unless you have the Moon in a water sign, like Scorpio. If you do, you will feel more at home with the depths of your partner's emotional realms. The two of you will be honest with each other, and will most likely enjoy diving into the caverns of the psyche as a means of churning up the details of the unconscious.

VIRGO–SAGITTARIUS (NOV. 22–DEC. 21)

Your character tends to be service-oriented with a keen awareness of your duties and responsibilities. You are exacting in the way you deal with the mundane tasks of everyday life and are a great asset at work and at home. The Sagittarius nature is dramatically different than yours, for they tend to be more broad-minded with sweeping goals and ambitions. Your Sagittarius partner is humorous, enthusiastic, and good-natured. He or she tries to make the best out of every situation. Under pressure, you focus on the little things, while the Archer aims the arrow of consciousness into the grand outer world. Your tendency may be to pull in to protect yourself in response to your mate's plans to travel or conquer the world. But if you can get past basic differences, the two of you can work effectively as a team, organizing the details of life with an open-minded awareness. Your chances for long-term compatibility are improved if the Moon in your chart is in a fire or air sign. If you can harmonize your wonderful potentials, the two of you should be able to enjoy the pursuit of shared social and intellectual activities with great interest and success.

VIRGO–CAPRICORN (DEC. 22–JAN. 19)

You're normally hesitant in your actions until you know that everything is proper. Your Capricorn lover is also conservative in action and carefully plans goals and then sets out to achieve them. You are both cautious about matters of the heart. As you tend toward critical thinking, you bring a sharp flavor of communication into relationships. To others, you can appear cool and distant. This works well with your Goat, for Capricorn is also well-guarded at the beginning of a relationship. Capricorns do not wear their heart on their sleeve and can hold back feelings until it appears very safe. Your partner is probably more serious than you are. If Venus in your chart is in Leo, you might find this seriousness too much. If your Venus is in Libra, you may not relate to Capricorn's belief that practicality is more important than beauty. In any event, your organizational abilities should blend nicely with Capricorn's ordered, but sometimes controlling, way of life. For the most part, you'll enjoy sharing the same space and can easily adjust to each other's habits. Romantic fires may take a while to get roaring, yet both of you can be very affectionate and sexy once you've moved past your issues of trust and have learned how to share.

VIRGO–AQUARIUS (JAN. 20–FEB. 18)

You have a very strong work ethics and are a service-oriented type of person. You have a deep desire to help others and are happiest when you're working efficiently at your tasks. Aquarius cares deeply about the greater community and is the humanitarian of the zodiac. Together, you can make waves and have an impact working with organizations, doing most any kind of group activity that involves high standards and shared values. That being said, there are some formidable differences. You are a practical, detail-oriented worker, whereas your Aquarius lover likes abstract intellectual principles. If you can stay open, Virgo, you stand to gain from the "big picture" that your Aquarius offers. If you aren't too critical, you can benefit from the many new friends that your partner brings into your life. If, however, you have Mars in a fire or air sign, then you may actually be as outgoing as your eclectic Aquarius mate. Ultimately, your Aquarius lover needs to relate with intelligent people, and you qualify on this account— you're not only a suitable mate, but your clear thinking can be quite inspiring to your partner. If nothing else, you two make compatible friends— of course, this compatibility can go much further.

VIRGO-PISCES (JAN. 20–FEB. 18)

Sometimes opposites do attract, and there's no doubt about it: Pisces is your opposite. You are exacting and disciplined where Pisces can be scattered and spacey. You are rational and logical while Pisces is imaginative and emotional. You respond to life's circumstances by narrowing your focus, analyzing the details as you figure out your next move. Your Pisces lover discards obvious facts while searching inward, relying on intuition instead of data. If the Moon in your chart is in a water sign, then you'll be more open to the imaginal realms of your Pisces. If the Moon in your chart is in an earth sign, you may think that Pisces is just too flaky for you. You may get annoyed at what you consider escapist tendencies in your lover, although he or she may not see it that way. If, however, you can accept your differences, you can actually be of great help to each other, as you each bring balance into the areas of life that are weak for the other. In fact, you can serve as mirrors to each other's souls. This relationship softens you and teaches you how to become more compassionate. You can teach your Fish how to productively organize his or her life. Together, you can be very sweet and loving.

ABOUT THE AUTHORS

RICK LEVINE When I first encountered astrology as a psychology undergraduate in the late 1960s, I became fascinated with the varieties of human experience. Even now, I love the one-on-one work of seeing clients and looking at their lives through the cosmic lens. But I also love history and utilize astrology to better understand the longer-term cycles of cultural change. My recent DVD, *Quantum Astrology*, explores some of these transpersonal interests. As a scientist, I'm always looking for patterns in order to improve my ability to predict the outcome of any experiment; as an artist, I'm entranced by the mystery of what we do not and cannot know. As an astrologer, I am privileged to live in an enchanted world that links the rational and magical, physical and spiritual—and yes—even science and art.

JEFF JAWER I'm a Taurus with a Scorpio Moon and Aries rising who lives in the Pacific Northwest with Danick, my double-Pisces wife, our two very well-behaved teenage Leo daughters, and two black Gemini cats (who are not so well-behaved). I have been a professional astrologer since 1973. I encountered astrology as my first marriage was ending. I was searching and needed to understand myself better. Astrology filled the bill. More than thirty years later, it remains the creative passion of my life as I continue to counsel, write, study, and share ideas with clients and colleagues around the world.

ACKNOWLEDGMENTS

Thanks to Paul O'Brien, our agent, our friend, and the creative genius behind Tarot.com; Gail Goldberg, the editor who always makes us sound better; Marcus Leaver and Michael Fragnito at Sterling Publishing, for their tireless support for the project; Barbara Berger, our supervising editor, who has shepherded this book with Taurean persistence and Aquarian invention; Laura Jorstad, for her refinement of the text; and Sterling project editor Mary Hern and designer Rachel Maloney for their invaluable help. We thank Bob Wietrak and Jules Herbert at Barnes & Noble, and all of the helping hands at Sterling. Thanks for the art and ideas from Jessica Abel and the rest of the Tarot.com team. Thanks as well to 3+Co. for the original design and to Tara Gimmer for the author photo.